DON'T STOP ME NOW

poetry and prose

Natalie Skorykova

Bambaz Press
Los Angeles 2023

Copyright ©2023 by Natalie Skorykova
All Rights Reserved
Printed in the United States of America

Book Design & Cover Art: Baz Here
Edited by Bambi Here

ISBN: 9798390417652

Bambaz Press
548 S Spring Street
Suite 1201
Los Angeles, CA
90013

contact: Bambi@bambazpress.com

2018-2022

[introduction]

2018. It was a year when I wrote texts from this book. It was a significant year: I met Jack, I found Method Writing, and I spent six months in LA.

Now it's 2022. I don't live in Ukraine. I live in the South of Spain. The man I loved and who you'll find in these texts is dead. Russia began the full-scale war in Ukraine.

I live alone in the village with two dogs. I have a sea view. I'm a teacher and I have students around the world.

A lot of things changed. But something remains unchanged—I write, and I want to write.

This book is my first step. My personal writing step. It's not perfect. It's not great. It is the first and I'm proud of myself because I remember how scary and challenging to make the first step.

And now, after I've done this first step, I don't want to stop.

-Natalie Skorykova

CONTENTS

POETRY

- BRING ME TO THE SEA 9
- WE COULD 11
- ON THE TOP 16
- THAT VESSEL 19
- NEW MOON TOMORROW 21
- THE CAGE 25
- THE GOLDEN SHADOW 29
- THE SHAKY GROUND 31
- INNER OCEAN 33
- MY OWN REMEDY 36
- THE CINEMA 38
- I AM AN ART 40
- CLIFFS 41
- BEGINNING 43

PROSE

- GOING ON 51
- THE BAR 56
- MR. MIST 59
- I NEED A GUN 62
- RED LION MASK 65
- ANIMALS' LIFE 69
- GREEN DOOR 72
- SUPERMARKET 75
- AGORA 77
- WALLS 81
- PUPPY 84
- FAULT 86
- EMPTINESS 89
- MY FATHER'S DAUGHTER 92
- MY MOTHER'S DAUGHTER 97
- FAREWELL 101

POETRY

BRING ME TO THE SEA

my love,
bring me to the sea.
my soles need to touch the sand
my cheeks miss the salty breeze
for a long time
my eyes haven't squinted from the sun
and the wind hasn't tangled my hair.

my love,
bring me to the sea.
my palms need to touch the waves
my ears miss the cry of gulls
for a long time
my lips haven't kissed the wind
and the sun hasn't burned my face

my love,
bring me to the sea
my soul needs to touch the blue horizon
my heart misses the clear night sky
for a long time
my body hasn't danced with surf
and my mind hasn't r grown up with the sun.

my love,
we have no ocean, no sea
no even little puddle.
dry land, grey asphalt, black flower beds
and yellow trees
brick buildings, curtains on the windows,
cars, trams, buses, and din.

my love,
can you see the horizon?
this yellow light
is from the lamp on our ceiling
we have no sky

my love,
we have no wind,
only the enveloping heat
of the AC

my love,
bring me to the sea
I miss the closeness

WE COULD

Stars, fears, faith and fates.
Who knows what really exists—
The stars, which create our fates?
The fears, which create our fates?
Or the faith, which creates everything
in this world?

We don't know why
we met like this
in that place,
at that time,
on that non-descript day,
a day like any other.
You were waiting for your Americano
with no milk—
I was waiting for my big Cappuccino
standing in line
in "Paul," the French café
in the heart of old Kyiv
on Yaroslaviv Val street.

People at the tables
rattling the cutlery.
Someone ate a croissant—
smearing it with raspberry jam
and soft butter.
Someone eating curd pancakes
dipped in a sour cream
sprinkled with powdered sugar.

It was morning
The usual morning
before work.
The usual breakfast
before the ordinary day.
The barista pounded the portafilter,

shook out the pressed coffee.
The waiter was wiping
the vacated table.

Smells of bread, pastry and coffee
teasing my nostrils
and enticing my stomach.

You stood by the window—
tall, confident, in a blue jacket
and purple waistcoat.
The jacket was buttoned
on the one wine-colored button.

A check fell on the floor.
Nobody noticed it.
Everyone trampled on it.
I picked it up
and you saw me.
Our eyes met.

Could you meet me
and simply let go?
Could I look at you
and not notice?

But now...

"We are star-crossed lovers.
It's the fault of the stars,"
we say.

What if it was
our fear that was at fault?
What if fear propelled us
to each other?
Neither work, nor travels,
nor family and money
could give us
what we were really looking for.

"To live and die without love"
propelled us to each other.
"To look in someone's eyes
in our own soul's reflection"
propelled us to find each other.

"To not feel who we are in this life"
propelled us
into this love,
in this fucking
complicated relationship.

We were afraid
to live with empty hearts.
We were petrified
of living with empty hearts.

Ships, shits, shields, and shifts.

The ship is full of shits,
shields, fears and faith
we call "The Life."
The life is full of shifts,
and we say "I didn't mean it.
I didn't expect it."
So, if we didn't—
if we didn't understand
why this love existed
then who managed that ship,
which we call "The Life."
Who captains this ship,
which we call "The Life."

Are we really so innocent?
You could meet me a
nd simply say nothing—
let it go,
forget
the way that long red scarf

I wore allowed just a nape
of my neck to show.
I could look at you
and not notice the color of your brown eyes
or your intense gaze upon me
as I was taking that Cappuccino.
That fucking Cappuccino.

We could.

A kind of selective blindness.

We could.
We can now.

But, you see,
we're like that ship.
We're full of shits,
shields, fears and faith.
We believe
that we have stars and fates.
We believe
that we can choose,
we believe
in love,
which will fill our sails
with the first fair wind that comes along.
And our ship—
though it be loaded and heavy
with past griefs and present obligations—
will just fly on the backs of those waves
that will carry us
to further seas and larger oceans
or crash
on the shore
of a deserted island.

We'll stand on the deck
and our eyes will reflect each other's souls.

We'll feel
who we are.

But we don't
and now,
there's no going back.

You put your phone
into your pants pocket,
you came into the café
in the heart of old Kyiv,
on Yaroslaviv Val street
where I was waiting for
my coffee
and you said,

"Is this your Cappuccino?

ON THE TOP

I'm going to my knees
For prayer.
I don't do that every day,
I don't do that usually,
I do it eventually.

And tonight, I want to pray.
Tonight, I want to kneel.

I don't know why I want to fall
down
It seems, sometimes I need it.
It's just an impulse.
Maybe,
I can't be on the top,
on this wooden floor
barefoot
in a white shirt and
blue skirt
Maybe,
I tend to be on the top.

On the top.

I scared
to be here.
I scared to lie down,
To fall
I scared to be
And not to be on the top of my life,
Of this life,
Tonight

I'm scared.

What is so terrifying here, in the middle?
Is it the middle?

The middle of my life?

I'm scared to be small.
I want to be big, outstanding and bright,
but I'm imperceptible.

"I stand, freeze...
And in the meantime - quiet, quiet
and sadly sings
something invisible"

I'm invisible. Hidden
on this wooden floor
barefoot
in a white shirt and
blue skirt

I'm scared to be on bottom.
I was there and I don't want
To be back.

I don't want to be empty,
To be devastated
by myself or others.
I don't want to be blasted, ruined.
I don't want to be destroyed
By parents, friends, society,

By lover.

By love and thoughts,
By feelings and experience.
I want to get rid of my demons.
They are so many and I'm alone.

I am the one.
On this wooden floor
barefoot
in a white shirt and
blue skirt.

I can be like a piece of glass
which some day may be a vase.

The flowers were inside,
The vase was part of celebrations,
It was a part of the house,
It was a part of family and generation.

I don't want to be a broken vase.

Splinters cannot be a vase.
The splinter, just one splinter
is always just a piece of something more.

I want to be this "more"

A vase, a plate, a picture,
chandelier on the ceiling
Even carpet at the door—
Or even be the door.

Debris, flotsam, slivers, threads, dry leaves, and dust—
Everything that lies on the ground,
Can no longer be of what it was.
What it should and has to be.
What it can be.

On this wooden floor
barefoot
in a white shirt and
blue skirt.

THAT VESSEL

Flash. Flesh. Flash.
Did you see that vessel?
Of course, you didn't.

Flash. Flesh. Flash.

The big, white seagull suddenly turns its head.
A lonely cashew lies on the beach in the ocean sand.
Tired, the cashew had been heated by the summer sun.

The big, white seagull spreads its wings.
It's being burned by the sun.
It can fly.
It has this ocean;
it has this ocean sand.
It hates other seagulls.

It saw that vessel.

Flash. Flesh. Flash.
Waves come and roll back out.

Surfs.
They're always here
In this ocean.
They kiss this ocean sand.
They watch the big white seagull.
They watch all seagulls.
They spit out the lonely cashew,
which had been heated by the smug summer sun.

They held that vessel.
The waves are always cold.
They're always here.
They always kiss.
They always hold.

Always kissing.
Always holding.
Flash! Flesh! Flash!

That vessel, which was out there—you didn't see.
"Where is it now?" asks the big, white seagull.
"It dead," says the small, grey seagull.
"How could you say that?" says, the big, white seagull.
"You didn't see it!"
"Who cares," the small, grey seagull says and takes the cashew.

Its orange beak with two black spots holds the tired cashew.
The summer breeze pets its grey feathers.
The waves kiss its black paws.

"Don't eat it!" the big, white seagull yells.
The small, grey seagull blinks and gulps down the cashew.
The small, grey seagull flies into the sky,
 into the distance.

"Flash. Flesh. Flash," the big, white seagull says.

The summer sky turns into the darkness.
The dark summer sky bursts with a flash and flesh.
Flesh, the small grey flesh, is under the waves.
The waves hold it with coldness.
The big white seagull stands on the warm ocean sand,
cold waves kiss its pink paws,
the summer breeze pets its white feathers.

Flash. Flesh. Flash.
No one has seen that vessel.

NEW MOON TOMORROW

I saw a young moon
with a lonely star.
They shone in the dark-blue sky.
They looked young and beautiful.
They looked like they appeared on the horizon
with the first leaf.

I thought,
tomorrow
they will be different.
I can't always trust the moon,
and sometimes the stars lie.
This will happen, they say;
but that happens instead.
I want this, but I get that;
I want today to last forever,
instead, it becomes tomorrow.

Tomorrow
things will be changed.
Tomorrow
changes me.
I know who I am—
tomorrow
I'm not what I was—
tomorrow
even if I do the same kiss.

What does exist
if nothing is permanent,
like a shell that breaks if I tap it too hard
with the same kiss?

I crossed the street.
I was waiting for an Uber.
I looked up at the night abyss
with the moon and the stars.

I looked at the sleeping city
and its sleeping, tricky, suspect bushes.
Nothing was unusual,
but the driver's name was Sky.
I saw her picture and her name
In the Uber app.

"How are you so far", she said
when I got in the car.
"I'm fine and you?" I said.
"I'm good", she said. "Are you visiting?"

Fuck. One phrase and she noted
I wasn't American.
Fucking accent—
stupid empty conversation!

"Where are you from?" she said.
"Ukraine... and you?" I said.

She was from Indonesia.

Ukraine and Indonesia
were riding in one car,
in the center of California,
in the city of Angels.

If we died at that moment,
It would be an international scandal.
If not a scandal—
just international news.
I hope it would be news.

International,
local American,
local Indonesian,
local Ukrainian—
it doesn't matter.

"I like your name", I said.

She told me
"It's my American name."
What was my name,
I thought,
my cargo?

What is my cargo,
I think?

Why am I Natalie?
Why am I not the news?
Why did I choose
my parents and my country?
Did I have a church?

No, I haven't.
I finished school,
I graduated from the University.
I have no institute.
I lost my persuasions
I lost other people's persuasions too.
I lost my dreams and goals.
I lost my reminiscences,
my thoughts,
my feelings,
my love,
my trust,
my confidence and impudence.

I lost.

All that I have is illusions.
Illusions and variants,
illusory variants
and variants of illusions.
Circle.
The Circle is not a church.
The Circle is the variants
that I pack.

Every day I stand at the crossroads
With the first leaf,
and bleeding soul and my iPhone.
I squint at the sun,
count the stars,
wish by the moon
and see what they offer.
"Who are they?"
I ask the eternal question.

I don't have an answer,
I have only variants and illusions how to think,
to decide
to believe,
to act,
to stop,
to cry
to love,
to die,
to live
and which Uber is mine.

I'm waiting for doves who cry.
White and grey they fly in the sky, fly in the sky,
not in the dark abyss
but in the blue clear sky
of the United States
of the Republic of Indonesia
of the Ukraine.

And the woman in the car looks at this sky
and says, "You will be Bride.
Someday.
Soon.
Maybe tomorrow."

THE CAGE

I'm sitting in an empty hotel room.
No matter how much furniture they have—
the bed, the desk, the tv, two chairs,
there's always that sense of emptiness.
It doesn't matter who designed the room,
how many tables, pictures, couches, magazines
they've crammed into that voluble space,
no matter how many stars are displayed
near the name of the hotel,
the emptiness lingers like a wet bedsheet
hung on the balcony line to dry in the sun.
I exit the bathroom and walk
smack into the wet sheet of emptiness.
I climb out of bed on a cold morning
and run smack into the wet sheet of emptiness.
I open the glass door looking out
onto the parking lot and step smack
into that wet sheet of emptiness
smelling of chlorine and soap.
These rooms belong to no one.
No soul seeps from the smell.
In ancient Greece everything had a touch soul—
tables, benches, trees, rivers, sandals, jugs.
But nothing had personality.
Those ancient Greeks had no definition for "personality." Drama gave
birth to "personal consciousness."
Sophocles gave birth to eye-gouging guilt and shame.
Personal consciousness replaced mythological consciousness.
Now, we are left with scraps of personality.
We've lost our souls.
Now, in order to have a soul,
we have to belong to something,
or to somebody.
Now, if we don't have faith,
we don't have soul.

We must belong to our faith.
It's not necessarily to believe in God.
The main thing is just to believe.
So, I'm sitting in this room which doesn't have a soul,
just a wet sheet of emptiness.
The button on my jeans presses into my belly,
my white t-shirt bites into my neck,
street sounds are muffled.
A lonely blackberry lies on the carpet.
I ate blackberries yesterday.
Three desk lamps give a soft faint light.
I don't know how people in the USA
live with no bright lights in the ceiling.
Perhaps, it's enough to be blinded by daylight.
But I need a bright light in my ceiling,
with this soft yellow night-light, I feel as if
I'm unable to examine myself,
unable to scrutinize myself.
I am shrouded by the darkness.
Sometimes, I want to be shrouded by darkness.
Sometimes, I need it.
My small hand, its tapered fingers
with remnants of red nail polish,
holds the room key.
My small hand holds the key.
My little hands hold the keys.
So many different keys,
keys to open so many doors.
I'm sitting in the shroud of this empty hotel room,
the muffled sounds of this city of angels.
But I can't hear the angels.
Only the muffled sound of the city.
Shrouded by the darkness, I think
«Я в клітці».
"I'm in клітка"
I don't know what's the word for "клітка" in English.
I opened a dictionary

and found that English had three different words for "клітка"
Three different cages,
three different types of cage:
cage for poultry—a coop.
Cage for a rabbit—a hutch.
It even had a special cage for a falcon—a mew.
In what cage was I?
In what cage am I now?
In a language cage.
It's strange, that English
doesn't have a special word for this type of cage.
I'm in a language cage
with the wet sheet of emptiness.
especially when I speak with him.
I've never felt it before like I felt it now.
I was in the situation
—in relationships I seem to have it all the time—
where I was misunderstood.
But now, I'm standing in this language cage
and I'm yelling,
I'm screaming,
"I need words, I want so many words!"
But I don't have it.
I can take them for free and I do it.
But to slowly, to slowly
God, how slowly it is!
How slow I am.
I need all those words inside of me.
But they lie outside
in books, in dictionaries,
in his heart and in the heart of his heart.
I want him to hear my words.
I want him to hear my heart
and the voice of the heart of my heart.
But he can only read them
because I can only write them.
It seems so simple, so easy,

but it's not.
When I write, I have time.
When I'm writing I have time to find the right word.
Right words.
Many different right words,
words which can open many doors
while I'm cooped up
in this empty room.

THE GOLDEN SHADOW

Yesterday I was reading about Apollo
as a god
and as an archetype of a human being.

Apollo is a god of the Sun,
a god of the arts,
(especially of music)
a god of prophecy and archery.
The golden child,
the beloved son of the great Zeus.

He is legislator and punisher.
He brings light and enlightenment.
He fights for truth and justice.
The entrance to his temple at Delphi
has his two main commandments—
"know yourself" and "know the measure."

On the one hand,
Apollo is a pure,
holy, purifying god.
The sun and the golden chariot
is harnessed with singing swans—
symbols of the light side of his magnificent personage.
On the other hand,
Apollo poses a dark side,
symbolized by a raven and a crow,
a snake and a wolf.

He did what he wanted.
He killed his mistress Koronis
for the crime of not loving him.
He exacted revenge on Cassandra
only because she rejected him.
He couldn't forgive.
He couldn't lose.

He had only his truth.

We forget about the dark side.
We forget about the shadow.
The foreboding shadow
of the golden Apollo—
about his vindictiveness
and cruel bloodthirst.

We forget about the dark side.
We forget about the foreboding shadow
of the human being,
the dark side of nature.

28-year-old golden Apollo,
a former machine gunner,
a decorated combat veteran
of the United States Marine Corps
killed 13 people.

California, the golden state,
the state of the sun,
the state of diversity, freedom,
and truth
incinerates the dwellings
of its own inhabitants,
ruining the lives of its people.

Dark side.
Shadow.

The glow of embers is beneath my feet,
my heels are burning,
my lungs are full of smoke,
devoid of oxygen to breathe—

my heart is shot.

Here is the shadow
of golden California.

THE SHAKY GROUND

I always feel a shaky ground
under my feet.
The shaky ground fills me with anxiety and dismay,
the shaky ground, like a quagmire,
grabs hold of my legs and hinders my movement,
the shaky ground bundles my thoughts with fishing twine,
knits knots, which I do not untangle,
twisting them ever more tightly
and I fall onto the shaky ground.

I'm trying in vain to take my next step
on the shaky ground.

I clamber, I suffocate,
I grab onto the branches of dry trees and young bushes,
I convince myself I can handle it,
and for a brief moment,
I even believe I can do it.
But then I slide down,
and collapse again,
onto the shaky ground,
and the trees with bushes watching silently
behind me.

I'm afraid to get stuck here.
I'm afraid to die here.
I am afraid of being rejected and not accepted.

Rejection and non-acceptance,
like heroin,
is ported through my blood by anxiety and dismay.
Rejection and non-acceptance,
like thin ice,
crunches under my feet, crackling;
and in that very moment
I reach an epiphany—
I'm mere seconds away

from plunging into the cold harsh water,
into the icy water, the dark water,
the lifeless water.

I'm afraid of being enveloped by this body of water
on the shaky ground.
Rejection and non-acceptance rule
as king and a queen over my life.
They compel me to adapt and serve,
they compel me into conformity and be silent.
They compel me to suffer in perpetuity.

Rejection and non-acceptance are born of love,
with the first love that writes from a clean slate,
a love that has no contradictions,
a love that does not ask,
a love that tells, compels,
like a king, like a queen.

My mother loved me.
She didn't beat me.
She was ignoring me.
She thought it would mold me into a better person.

Onto the shaky ground.

I compare myself with others.
I know it's like making new cuts
on my wrist
every day
and losing blood
slowly.

I convince myself
I can handle it,
and for a brief moment,
I even believe I can do it.

INNER OCEAN

I can't speak anymore.
I open my mouth,
but the words won't come.

I stand here,
in silent, on the sand,
looking out at the great ocean
before me,
the greater ocean
inside of me.
The soundless mood takes me over.

Yesterday, I finished reading Elena Ferrante's
first novel in her Neapolitan series.
I was reading until 4 am.
I kept the windows open.
I could hear the sound of the waves.
When I finished the book,
I was filled with my own solitude.
It's a stoic mood of being between two lives—
the one I'm living,
and the one out there,
beyond the sand
deep into Pacific Ocean
that tugs at me—
an ocean on which I might sail
into my unknown future
or drown caught in my unworkable present.

I will start her second book
looking for clues.
Maybe Elen, maybe Lila,
will show me the way?

I'm in this stoic mood.
There are so many amazing things
around me

and at the same time,
there are so many things
that I want to change
that I don't want
and I must accept.

My lover called to say
he couldn't come to see me.
Then he changed his mind
and decided to come.
We'll speak.
The words will come out
of my mouth,
the words will come out
of his mouth,
and I'll set sail or drown.

It is raining.
A thunderstorm rips up the sky's belly
and the sun shines brightly.
I'm not cold,
it's warm here,
but I'm all wet.
The clothes stick to my body
and I'm tired of walking through the rain.

All that remains for me to do
is simply walk.
Don't stop walking.
Continue on my way.

I walk along the sand and say nothing.
This life right now,
a quiet walk on the seashore,
the shifting sand beneath my feet,
the thunderous ocean rolling up
on this shore as I walk.

I imagine others enjoying dinner

with their families,
telling jokes,
recounting familiar stories of the past,
making plans for a seaside vacation
or a mountain retreat in the future.
It's right,
it's what should be.
But I?
Now, at this moment,
I'm with the ocean,
but I'm so lonely and dejected.
In some sense,
the ocean is inside of me.
I under its influence
I grow the ocean inside of me.

And to you, dear reader,
I send these little kisses
from the disappeared one,
who may or may not
be found—
who may be finding herself
by being lost
on an island that, like herself
waits for rescue.

MY OWN REMEDY

I lie down and cry—
scream and crawl
through the darkness of my world.
Like a horse, I give the coarse laugh.
Like a rooster, I screech to my mornings.
Like a snake, I hiss to my foes.
My cramps crack and burst at the seams.
My borders crumble disappears
in the fog through the darkness of my world.
I scream my whisper.
I crawl on my own spikes.
I choke my tears.
I sink my fears.
I sink my tremble.
The bricks crash against the ground
through the darkness of my world.
I fuck up. I fail. I fall down
on the boulders of my thoughts.
The tiger of purgatory tears my flesh.
His desire purges my sins.
His desire torments my soul
Forefather ghosts observe my defeat.
"You are the loser."
I am the loser?
I am the loser!
I crush.
Dry dust
on the wet cold old walls.
Vultures.
Hard beaks waiting for my sacrifice.
"No," I whisper through the darkness of my world.
"No!" I scream in their filthy blurry faces.
Torment me! Rape me. Destroy me.
Condemn me with your past.
Threaten me with your future.

Peck me with your decrepit prejudices.
Your roots are my roots.
Your blood is my blood.
Your history is my history.
But your actions, your gestures, your stirs are yours—
Not mine.
And your spirit has sunk into oblivion
 and created me.
This earth created me.
My eyes are full of blood.
My faith is the ether.
My cells store memory,
but the tiger has torn my flesh.
That tiger with fluorescent eyes
with claws like a bird.
I flattered him.
I remember his smell.
The smell of ash, death, fire, and doom.
The smell of fresh green spring grass,
plucked by children's hands,
hands smelling of vanilla cookies and warm milk.
And that tiger smelt like that.
Do not pounce on me.
You couldn't get me.
You tried to fuck me, and you fucked me,
but you didn't get me.
I got myself.
I cured myself.
I am my own remedy.

THE CINEMA

I can be alone and safe
in the cinema,
at the cinema.
it can be my shell, cave, and home real or imaginary.
It can be my refuge, shelter, escape, and trench;
I can hide there
in the cinema,
at the cinema.
I can be free,
I can be angry,
I can be abused
I can abuse
in the cinema,
at the cinema.
I can be the victim, aggressor, tyrant, megalomaniac,
mother, girlfriend, lover, wife, goddess
in the cinema,
at the cinema.
I'm justified in my tears;
I can live the life of a stranger;
I can ponder over my existence
to discover who I could and couldn't be
in the cinema,
at the cinema.
I can gorge myself on popcorn in the cinema.
It tastes better than home.
I can loudly gulp my Coke
at the cinema with no one to bat an eyelid.
I can laugh out loud even when the movie is sad.
I can sleep.
I can surf Facebook
at the cinema and no one would bat an eyelid.
No one bats an eyelid
in the cinema,
at the cinema.

I can waste my time.
I can waste my whole life
in the cinema,
at the cinema.
You can go with me to the cinema.
We can be together,
in the cinema,
at the cinema.

I AM AN ART

I'm not a woman, I am an Art
Each day makes some new strokes
Each day I think it's final touches
And then the dawn comes

I'm not a woman, I am an art
I possess different layers
I retain thousands of ideas of
Who and what I should,
I must be

I'm not a woman, I am an art
That's why I'm so expensive
That's why not everyone
Can read, can see, can feel
and understand me

I'm not a woman, I am an art
That's why you longing me
That's why I'm so free
That's why I'm so lonely

I'm not a woman, I am an art.

CLIFFS

My past is my prop.
It doesn't lead me.
God forbid to use the past
As a leader.

My past is many stones.
I built pavements, walls, parapets,
stone benches, statues, and gazebos.
I built parks, squares, fairgrounds and gardens.
Rock beds, tables, chairs, and fountains.
I look back. I see the city.
City of my past.

My past is full of lives.
It has love, hatred, and greed,
faith in God, in myself
and the complete destruction of the living.
It has a passion and cold,
fidelity and betrayal,
ascension to a deity and degradation to a worm,
which I trample into the ground or smear against
a stone pavement
after heavy rain.

My past is a stick.
I rely on it,
but I never look on it,
so as not to trip over branches,
so as to see my way,
I look straight ahead.
The stone city behind me.

Ahead of the mountains, rivers,
plains and thousands of cliffs.

Cliffs.
They are of different heights.

Some of them are inconspicuous.
I jump between them,
from one coast to another.
I forget and don't think
about the stick in my right hand.
I have legs and imaginary wings
of a large, colorful butterfly.

I am not a fairy,
I have no illusions about this.
Personally, I'm not good at magic.
I can't heal a person or make one fly,
I can't order the underwater rivers
of Africa to get out of the ground.
Rains, hurricanes,
they also don't obey me.
I can't teach one to sing.
Personally, I don't know how to sing.
I have the regular legs of a fragile woman
and the imaginary wings of a large, colorful butterfly.

And I jump
from one coast to another.

But there are steep cliffs.
A lot of them.
Below them is the abyss.
It takes my breath and sometimes paralyzes me;
It's hard to take a step
while standing on the edge of a high cliff.

I hold the stick tighter in my palm.
I look ahead to the mountains, rivers,
plains and thousands of cliffs.
And I jump.

BEGINNING

I'm 17.
He looks at me,
into my eyes.
He asks with a gaze,
I answer him with a silent,
"Yes."

He takes off my little panties.
Now he's kissing me.
We both are naked.
He leaves.

I look in the mirror.
Yes, I see myself,
examining my body—
my face flushed,
the nipples became hard,
the tangle of pubic hair is wet.
When did my girl's body change like this?
Before, it was a girl's body,
now I am looking at the body
of a young woman.
The little girl here looks in the mirror
in the body of a young woman.
I claim it, the little girl claims
her woman's body.
I say a silent, "Yes."

I look at the crumpled sheets.
I see the smeared stains of blood.
And I think—
yes, it's just the beginning.

I'm 21.
I live in Kryvyi Rih,
founded as a postal city in 1775
by Cossacks, now the main steel-industry

city of Eastern Europe.
I move from Kryvyi Rih for Kyiv.
I leave my job.
I leave my boyfriend.
I'm alone in the city of Kyiv,
founded in the late 9th century
but going back to the late paleolithic period
when the first humans made Upper Paleolithic art.

I don't have safety.
I don't have stability.
I don't have money.
I don't have love.

All I have is independence.
I have no idea
what the future will bring.

I'm standing on the roof.
I see the night lights of the city of Kyiv,
this cultural center of Eastern Europe.
The river Dnipro flows southward
toward the Black Sea.
In the distance, I can see
the lights on the Maidan Nezalezhnosti.
The lights which seem to be asking me.
I answer those lights with a silent,
"Yes."
And I think—
It's just the beginning.

I'm 25.
I'm a top manager.
I have safety
I have stability.
I have money.
I have independence.

I don't have love.

And I have no idea
what the future will bring.

I'm looking at my lover,
who I don't love.
I see my phone,
hear a call coming in.
It's from the office,
which I hate.
We are sitting at the restaurant
which he likes.

Later, on the red sofa,
Christina Aguilera sings "The Voice Within."
My lover asks,
"Do you really want to break up with me?"
I answer him with a silent,
"Yes."
And I know—
It's just the beginning.

I'm 27.
My love holds my hand.
We are sitting in our new apartment
on the yellow sofa.
Etta James sings "At Last"
and he looks at me,
into my eyes.
He loves me.
I love him.
It's all so simple.

We'll make paleolithic art
between us and life will be fine.
He says, "You can leave your job.
You can trust me.
I will take care of you."
I can hear the river cutting its way
through the center of the city,

on the right bank the woody hills,
ravines, and smaller rivers.
Come winter, parts of the reservoir locks
will be frozen over.
I answer him with a silent,
"Yes."

I have safety.
I have stability.
I have money.
I have love.

I lose independence
and I have no idea
what the future will bring.
But I think it's just the beginning.

I'm 30.
I'm in L.A.,
the City of Angels,
bounded on one side by the Pacific Ocean,
and on the other by mountains
as high as ten thousand feet.
I'm trying to become a writer.
A good writer.
I'm standing on the hotel balcony.
In the distance
I can see the Hollywood Sign.
I squeeze a piece of paper
fresh with a poem.
I'm worried that my poem is bad.
My poem is empty.
Nothing flows through it,
no paleolithic art,
just frozen reservoir locks.
I worry.
I'm empty.
I'm bad.

I will never be a writer—
a good writer.

He looks at me,
into my eyes.
I know him,
but at the same time
I feel I have never known him,
nor will I ever know him.
"I love you," he says.
"I love you, too," I say.
But we have no idea
what the future will bring.

We see the night lights of L.A.
It answers us with a silent
"Yes, it's just the beginning."

I am
I don't know how old I am.
I'm lying in my bed.
I see the night lights of a night city,
but I don't know the name of the city.
Buildings in the distance
with no name on them,
no one knows when the city was founded,
no one knows what rivers, if any,
will run through it, what mountains, if any,
will rise up from the earth.

This is the city I should live in.
A city unbound by anything.
But I don't know.
It's hard to remember.

I have safety.
I have stability.
I have money.
I have love.

I have independence.
I'm a good writer.

I'm look at the ceiling
and think
I have no idea
what the future will bring.
But
 I'm happy.
I can whisper.
I can whisper what I feel.
And I'm whispering with a silent yes.
"Yes, it's just the beginning.
It's always an eternal beginning."

PROSE

GOING ON

It's September 19th, 2018.

Late last night, I saw a young woman standing on the beach in Santa Monica. She was wearing a gray hooded gym outfit. The sky and ocean stood as a black backdrop, the universe of stars above us. Her hair was blown about by the wind coming off the ocean. Just north of her, the lights on the big Ferris Wheel from the Santa Monica Pier Amusement Park cast a series of colors, shadowing her face. The red shadow was from its heart; the blue and yellow ones came from the big smiling grin on the wheel as it turned slowly against the force of the wind; the green shadow from its rings circled her body, and a turquoise shadow jumped across her body from its flickering lights. She had been talking to the ocean. I see lots of people here at night talk to the Pacific Ocean. I've talked to the ocean myself. I know, he loves me. All the oceans love me.

She tells the ocean, plain and simple: I'm going. I'm going on. I'm going on along the sand.

I'm going along the cold sand. It doesn't burn my feet. Summer's long gone, like a thief in the night. Hightailed it out of here. The summer has left this sand and left me, as well. We're both cold, the sand and I, but we're still here. We're going on. The dark sky above us, lit by a scattering of stars, lights from the Ferris Wheel thrown like confetti onto the inky blackness—stare at those stars long enough and they begin to shine for you. I know, the ones that twinkle are stars, the ones that aren't planets. There's Venus, just above the horizon. There's Mars, that smudge of orange from the Red Planet. There's Jupiter, the biggest star in the sky, or maybe it's Saturn, she never learned to tell the difference. That slight bulge, maybe those are the rings. Where's their winter or summer when you need them. They have no winter or summer. So far from the sun, they limp across the night sky oblivious to that girl, to her pain, to the cold sand beneath her feet. Probably, that's why they always shine, she thought. Nothing to get hung about, strawberry fields forever. It was all so easy when she lived with eyes closed, when nothing was real, when she misunderstood all she saw, then no one but she was in her tree.

But now I'm going down, I'm going on, strawberry fields forever. Maybe that's why that girl in the gray hoodie preferred the Pacific Ocean. It's always cold, it's always going on, rolling great waves outward toward the black night, up to the planets and stars hung like fruit you feel you can reach out and pluck. There seems no reason to stay alive, even, when you know—someday you'll die.

"I'm still alive," she whispers.

Did she know I was listening, watching her, standing on the edge of this planet, this earth?

The moon kept me chained with its gaze. Even when the summer left me and the earth is cold, I chose to go on.

It's July 21st, 1911.

Germany sends warships to Agadir threating a new European war. British seamen go on strike. Heat records are set all across American, 113 degrees in Junction City, Kansas.

In Kyiv, the horse's hooves clopping on the round paving stones of the streets. In Kyiv, it's also hot day. It smells of linden, those cordate leaves with their wing-like bracts, those petite yellow petals that hang like tears, most of them now covering the streets. The rare wagon's wheels creak. Horses snort, chewing their metal snaffles. Summer city dust hangs in the air.

I see a woman. She's sitting on the stairs of the Karaite synagogue. She's dressed in a white volumetric lace blouse with a dark heavy long skirt. Her hair is braided. A light breeze moves some strands out of her hair and plays with them. The dark façade of The Karaite Kenesa of Kyiv in the Moorish style embraces her. It hides her from noise and dust, from linden tears and playful wind. She is sitting and she is writing. Her left arm is crippled. She is constantly in pain. The pain drives her to the sea and the ocean. The pain says to her, "It will be easier for me there, I'll rest, and I'll leave you behind."

She is writing:
Lukash: "How long have you lived in this world?"
Mavka: "Actually, I've never thought about that. . . . It seems to me, I've lived forever. . . ."
Lukash: "And were you always just the same as now?"
Mavka: "It seems, I've been the same. . ."

She takes her writing. She meets her man. She stands up and goes. I look at them as they walk away. She holds his arm. She walks with the pain. But she goes and she goes on.

It's October 21st, 1928.

I'm 30. I have a husband and two kids. My husband is a Fellow of the College at the University of Cambridge. Today I was in the university's garden with him and our kids. I was watching a woman. She was sitting on the banks of a river.

To the right and left bushes of some sort, golden and crimson, glowed with the color, even it seemed burnt with the heat, of fire. On the further bank the willows wept in perpetual lamentation, their hair about their shoulders. The river reflected whatever it chose of sky and bridge and burning tree, and when the undergraduate had oared his boat through the reflections they closed again, completely, as if he had never been.

She was alone. I was looking for her man or friend, but I saw she was alone.

What is her name? I thought. I could call her Mary Beton, Mary Seton, Mary Carmichael. Or by any other name—it's not a matter of any importance. I wish I could sit as she did. I wish I could be alone as she was. My husband had met his friend from the university. They were speaking. I held the two kids' hands. Their little warm hands were sweaty, dust clinging to their palms. Emily caught a ladybug. It flew in and landed on her collar. Emily took it and squeezed it into her small fist. Tomas was hunting for a large unknown beetle. It was swift and quickly hid in the grass and leaves. My kids wanted to run. They wanted to run along that soft, bright, autumn grass filled with beetles. But they couldn't do that. None of us could do that. For us, I mean, for kids and women, men had created special rules. We couldn't run. We couldn't have our own beetles. And certainly, we couldn't run along the grass—not the grass all manicured in that part of the university. We couldn't be by ourselves.

That woman stood up and went along the grass lawn. What was she doing, I thought, is she crazy? Instantly a man appeared to intercept her. His face expressed horror and indignation. He was a Beadle; and she was a woman. Of course. She was definitely crazy. I didn't hear his voice, but I knew what he was telling her. She had to leave the well-manicured lawn.

She had no right to go the way she wanted. She had to go the long way, around the statue, around the big oak trees, around the medical building, around the parking lot, around everything but the path she was on.

My husband had finished his conversation. We had to go. Home. I didn't want to, but I went. I always go, I always go on.

Thirteen years later, when World War II kidnapped my son and destroyed my daughter's youth; when I forgot how the voice of my husband sounded (he kept silent and just read his newspapers), my neighbor told me that there was this one woman who went to the river Ouse and didn't come back. I thought it was the same woman that I saw at the university of Cambridge. She had enough courage to sit alone by the river; she had enough courage to leave; she had enough courage not to come back. It was an overcast night. The sky was wrapped in thick clouds like a mummy's bandage. Nature tried to keep peace on the top. That was how nature tried to save its haven.

I didn't see the stars. I didn't see the moon, but I felt her. I know the moon is female. I know she exists, and she is a goddess. She was here before us. She's here with me now. She watches me. And she will be here when I go away, when all of us will go away.

That girl on the Santa Monica beach, what was her name? I could call her Mary Beton, Mary Seton, Mary Carmichael— I's not a matter of any importance. Her name doesn't have a meaning. Her name doesn't have a history. Yet, inner cramps, the spirits of the past, choke from the inside. They remind me of who she was.

I can freely walk along the sand, along the green grass in any corner of this world. My sky is clear; I have the stars and her. But I feel that before I was unable to walk; before my body ached, my soul was ill; before I learned how to endure, how to succumb and how to be silent... and how to break the rules.

Two invisible wings, the spirits of the future, give her courage. They remind her of who she wants to be. I have enough courage to be here alone; I have enough courage to stand on the edge of the earth; I have enough courage to leave; I have enough courage not to come back. She always goes. She goes on. The path lies before me. She's watching me. She watched the others. I watched them all. I'll be watching them until they go on. Until they follow the path that lies before them.

I feel the breeze, the wind, not from the ocean, but from those wings, beating furiously behind me.

THE BAR

"Sorry." he said. There were two glasses on the sticky brown bar counter. The one with transparent white liquid was hers: a double shot glass of gin; the second with a dark brown liquid, was his: whiskey, the same brown color as the bar counter. If you weren't careful, you could end up drinking the countertop as well.

"I don't like the way things are," she said. A song, no? The way things were. The way we were. Redford and Streisand. Prep sweaters. Quaint world of revolutionary agitation. Agit-Prop. Stalin. Putin. Babyn Yar. The dead out of graves stalking the world.

Her fingers with purple nails held a white paper napkin. A spot of the ketchup on the bar was waiting to become a part of her blue jean jacket. I kiss my father. Blue lips on red lips in the freezing cold of Kyiv. Dog bites. Little puppy my mother disapproves of.

"But that's the way they are." he said. He. The man. The man who never changes. Mother spitting the words out, I am the thing she spitted out. I am spit; I am out. I exude from other people's pores, phlegm, mucus, sputum. He. The man. Barricades of ships that line the river that cuts the city in half. Conjugate the word. Fuck. Fucked. Had been fucked. Will be fucked. I am fucked in the fuck of the fuck. I say the word, it consumes me. I want to be fucked, but not fucked up. His nostrils didn't notice how they inhaled cigarette smoke. There was a time when he used to breathe cigarette smoke. One cigarette after another, chain smoking from dawn to bedtime, and even in the middle of the night when he couldn't sleep. Fresh air seemed abnormal. At 2pm, every day, he drank a single shot of whiskey, savoring the taste of its malted grain, the barley, the corn, the rye, the wheat, aged in barrels, some for just a few years, some for decades. Whiskey from Ireland, whiskey from Scotland, whiskey from Canada, whiskey from Tennessee. I didn't want to change my life just because she was careless and had gotten pregnant, he thought. After all, it was her body, and this was his life. He couldn't make those two lives congruent. It was one life or the other.

"Hey, would you look at that?" she said, because the silence between them was killing her. It was sticky the same as that bar counter impregnated with cheap alcohol and dirty rags. An old woman outside the window was beating an old man with her bag and frantically screaming.

"I have never seen anything like it," he said with a smile. His dirty, baggy jeans were held up by a belt. The button had come off two or four weeks ago and since then, the button remained in the left back pocket. He could feel it whenever he sat down. Pocket button, button belt. Button up your overcoat. A belt in the mouth. I belt the drink down. We drove the beltway in Washington. We went in circles. I'm going in circles, spit and shit and babies born like shit through my open legs.

"It reminds me of something, though," she said. The aluminum ring on her right ring finger reminded her of that August evening when he had given it to her. When he left, she stood in front of the mirror and imagined that it was a golden ring with a huge diamond. Her grandma, when she saw the ring, said, "It's all he can afford and you're a silly girl who thinks that he will change. Remember, men never change." I watched her spit on the threshold of our dilapidated house a block from the factory that made auto parts. The spittle pooled onto the floor, a drop of brown sputum the size of a quarter. Those were its two options, she thought: to be dry or to be rubbed onto the sole of someone's shoe. My life has been reduced to an option. Do I make the choice or am I the choice? Circles. 5'clock shadows. Tsvetaeva wrote about Pushkin: "All the things of my life I loved and kept on loving through parting, but the sea is tomorrow, the sea was between us, the whole blue sea of delaying, the whole blackness of night kept on coming to me alone," like a lover's orgasm, the fucked up sea of regret.

"Do you remember the house at the end of Cedar Street?" he said.

No, she wanted to say, but she didn't. She didn't want to remember that house. She wanted to yell, but she didn't. She felt nausea rise up from her stomach. This gin, this dirty bar, those cold French fries and sour ketchup made her nauseous. His blue empty eyes, his rough calloused hands, his empty rough heart made her sick.

"Yeah" she said and took a sip of the gin, let the alcohol remain in her throat until it stinged her gullet, then swallowed, feeling the needles all the way down.

Look, I don't want you and your stupid child, he wanted to say, leave me alone. I don't like how you smell; I hate how you whine and scratch my back while I'm fucking you! But he held the words in, held them in like nails gouging his chest from the inside. Aloud, he calmly said, "Why?"

She sees his profile. She sees his crumpled checkered plaid shirt. She sees the dirt under his fingernails. She sees her own reflection in the mirror behind the bar, showcasing those bottles of Jim Beam and Canadian Club, Jack Daniels, Johnny Walker Red, Old Crow, Old Forester, Fighting Cock and Wild Turkey, Maker's Mark, George Dickel, Crown Royal, Seagram's Seven, Gunpowder Rye and Northern Light. She imagined herself in the mirror wearing a blindfold, hands tied behind her back, and each bottle holding a rifle aimed at her heart. "No reason" she said.

There was that salty taste of his own blood in his mouth. The lip cracked again. The juke played "This is the road to hell," by Chris Rea. All this life is the road to hell, so why give birth and life if it was all the same and all there was to do was die.

"Maybe we'd better just both go home," he said, but she knew, neither of them had a home. They both lived as ghosts. She didn't want to be a ghost. She knew, there was a real life outside. A life that didn't stink of cigarettes and alcohol. There she wouldn't be just a reflection in a mirror behind a row of whiskey bottles. I'll change my life. I'll change my destiny for this child, growing inside of me. Growing for my future; I won't be dry, and I won't be rubbed onto the sole of someone's shoe. She lifted the glass of gin, took the last sip, all of it, and set the glass back down on the table so hard it nearly broke. But it didn't.

MR. MIST

Today I have been eating, writing, deleting, and sleeping. I cleared my mail from the spam, and it felt as if I had unloaded a truck, one box at a time. Now, I'm looking out of the picture window of my apartment at the beach and the ocean stretching far out toward the horizon, and beyond that, Japan. A thick fog rises up from the ocean. By tonight, you won't be able to see your toes wiggling in the sand. I live on the last floor, my windows at the back of the building. On a clear day, I can see the beach and the ocean. But today, the thick mist, and then the fog, like the breath of a malevolent being seeping its way into my apartment, into the pores of my skin, finding a way to enter my throat if I opened my mouth to breathe. I don't open my mouth; I don't breathe. I just look out at the thick mist with those small yellow lights inside of it.

It reminds me of my first apartment which I had just one window with the view on the brick wall. It was like an apartment for blind people, an apartment for blind and lonely woman. But I wasn't blind. I was lonely and I was poor with no money, no profession and no hopes. Did it mean the same as the blindness meant? Can I say that now, in this apartment with the ocean view and a lover, who says, "I love you?" I'm a sighted person. Can I?

This fog makes me feel blind. I open the windows which keep everything from entering my apartment, the feelings of solitude and loneliness.

When I open the window, in comes Mr. Mist and in comes the feelings of being alone. The ocean stretches all the way to Japan just steps away. The ocean that allows the small arms of Mr. Mist to rise into this room. He seeps into this room on those little cat feet that Sandburg talked about. Mr. Mist holds me here on the last floor and it seems like he takes me up. He holds me blind and lonely on this beige couch.

Eliot's "Fisher King" sits in the mist, barren and sick. I'm sitting with him on my beige couch and we both in the Unreal City under the brown fog a winter dawn.

My mother had one man in her life, and I have my solitary lover, who leaves me every day to secure cyber space from the disease of the world. He gives me to Mr. Mist.

I fell asleep. I saw an odd dream where reality mixes up with dreams.

I saw children. They had been running on the beach and greeting Mr. Mist—they said, "Hello." And he smiled at them. Then I saw these children running out from the Soviet kindergarten. It was April 26th, it was 1986, I wasn't born yet, but I already existed, and I saw children and I saw him, Mr. Mist. He looked at me. He said, "Hello."

It seems that Mr. Mist has been mixing it up. It seems he is mixing everything up. He's a trickster, a playful sprite, like Puck in Midsummer Night's Dream. It's no longer midsummer, it's the end of summer, it's the beginning of fall. I will fall into another winter, maybe the winter dawn.

Yesterday Mr. Mist kissed me. I was blind and thought that my lover kissed me.

Today I'm the sighted person. Today I find out that the fastest animal on the planet in English sounds like a monkey. I'm shocked and disappointed. Cheetah.

I am Natalie, I am Skorykova.

Maybe the name doesn't matter. The name, it's just words: гепард, cheetah, Acinonyx jubatus. Nature doesn't connect with the stupid names we give it. Nature connects with its essence.

I must find my essence. I want it. I need it. I am bound by the name that I think defines me. I'm Natalie, I'm Skorykova, that's how they call me—Natasha, Natashulka, Nataha, Natashka, Natalka, Tatka.

Mr. Mist makes all the human noise I hear from the Santa Monica Pier quieter. Those sounds of people crying from the top of the roller coaster, the top of the Ferris wheel where they can see the land and the ocean. All is disappearing into the mist. No wonder they scream, no wonder they cry. Meanwhile, Mr. Mist makes the noise of the ocean. I'm in his invisible hands.

I wish he could be here, now, my friend and lover, my life partner, my other being. He is away doing his work out in the world. He sleeps in another bed; he sees another view from the window. We look through the different windows.

He sleeps with another woman.
He betrays three of us.
I betray myself.

I want to go outside, but I'm scared—so many odd men who want to speak with me, who ask me questions, who want something from me. How odd it is that in Ukrainian, "odd" means "hell." The odd men break my boundaries. I don't want to speak.
I am safe inside this apartment. I am safe inside a cave.
I am trapped.

I NEED A GUN

Can you believe? Two weeks and not a single note. Of course, I want to say it's his fault. I mean, every time when he comes, I feel like I'm falling. I come down in another world. His world. You get my drift? I live with my own schedule, I have my own routine and then he comes and as vacuum, sucks me into his world. I'm telling you, I'm not a dust to be sucked by all sorts of vacuum cleaners! Am I right or am I right?

Ok, yes, he's not a vacuum. I'm a child and he's like parent. He is the father or the mother, he's both. And I'm that little girl who must eat fucking oatmeal. By the way, I don't know why every time when I want to say something unpleasant about my parents, I talk about oatmeal. I mean this is the part that's really weird. My parents didn't stuff me with oatmeal. Thank them. Lucky me. What they really did, they compelled me to eat honey. Yes, you heard right, honey, the fucking honey made by the fucking angry bees. I hate bees and their healthy shit until this day. Do you feel me? I know, it's not the bees' fault; it's my parents' fault. I mean, when I was a child I couldn't say, "Hey, Mom, I don't want to eat this fucking shit. Eat it by yourself, ok?" Of course, I tried to say something like that, but you know, when your parents wanted your "yes" and you said them your indignant "no", they weren't ceremonious, they were giving you a slap and you were doing all that they needed.

So, anyway, like I was saying, when he comes, I turn into that good girl who does everything that her parents expect. Did I tell you? I hated slaps! Maybe, that's why I was a very good girl, a perfect daughter, I'm dying if I'm lying. Poor brother. By the way, yes, I have a brother. He is 11 years older than me. I remember, when he was at 10th grade, it means, he was 16 or 17 and I was, let me count… fucking calculators! Fucking scientific and technical progress! I can't quickly say how much is 17 minus 11! And all because when I was in 5th grade, I had the calculator. Now we all have calculators in our phones, cell phones. A little bit more and we'll not able to wipe our ass without a phone. So, where was I? Ah, my brother was 17 and I was 6. He went to a school tour in Sevastopol. How much shit happened during this time. I mean, I grew up, my brother now is 40 years old man, and these scums took the Crimea. When I was 6 and my brother was 17, the Crimea was an autonomous republic and schoolchildren from all over the former Soviet Union were going on excursions and rest in the Crimea. And now what? I'm telling you; this world is going to the hell and we're going with it. But when my brother was 17 and I was 6, the world was better. Believe me, I know what I'm saying.

When he came back from that school tour to Sevastopol, he brought me a gift. He bought two BB guns. You know that big plastic gun with small plastic bullets. My brother was a very kind boy, that's why he bought one BB gun for himself and one for his lovely little sister. To say I was happy means to say nothing. Do you follow me? I mean, when you're 6 and your little hands hold BB gun you feel like you're fucking Superman! I was a fucking Superwoman. Do you know why? Because when you're a cute little girl, when you're your father's princess you can do a lot of different things, bad things, of course, only nerds and geeks want to do good things, normal children think about poop, how to hurt someone, how to steal something and other shit like this. Of course, when you're small you do that unconsciously. Although... Ah, it doesn't matter. Where was I? Oh, I was a 6-year-old princess with BB gun. Remember, I told you, my brother was poor. Believe me, he was. Before we started to play with him with those plastic guns, I saw a superb movie—"Rambo. First Blood." Lake little Rambo, I hid under the cover on my parents' bed and when my brother, my imaginary enemy came into the room, I jumped out under the covers and shot him. Point-blank!

Oh man, I'm telling you, it was such a good time. You know what, I got it! I need a BB gun. No, I need a real gun to shoot the hell out of all my imaginary enemies. Do you know what I mean? Do you feel me? I mean so much shit sits in this world and in my head. I'm 30 years old and some people still make me feel like my father's 6-year-old princess who can't say "no" to parents and who can fire at her brother with the gun just because she saw Rambo and it was fun.

How much shit we've done just because it was fun. How much shit we do just for fun. What is going on here? I mean I see some people who are 50, 60, 70 years old and they behave like children. Are there any adults on this planet or we're just old children who play adult's games? Am I right or am I right? I'm telling you, this world is going to the hell and we're going with it. Fuck it. I have to go. I have to write something, some new piece of shit. Where's my gun? My real gun...

RED LION MASK

They promised to give me my Red Lion.

I thought it was a red dragon, but the chef explained to me that it was a Japanese Red Lion. When I first saw it, I mean, my Red Lion, I felt it should be mine. I wish I could always feel what exactly should be mine.

The chopstickrest hashioki was lying on the table; the sun was lying on the table at the Sushi Ginza Onodera restaurant. I put my palm on it; I made an eclipse; I closed my eyes and switch on the light.

"Could I buy this Japanese Red Lion?" I asked a waitress.

The drawn curtains absorbed the sound of quiet voices. No music, no talk, just rustling, like a ghost, a whisper. The blade of the Yanagi-ba slid over the flesh of a dead fish. It was Hamachi, or how Europeans and Americans say, Yellow Tail. We all hoped it died recently; some of us wanted it to be still alive.

Yanagi-ba and Shobu, two Japanese fish knives are literally a willow leaf and an iris leaf. Thin, steel, sharp leaves, they cut the fish flesh, and we absorb it. Aesthetic pleasure—the pleasure of death, where the main thing is that it should be beautiful, with leaves and cut to the quick.
Cool sake in lacy cups kiriko threw shadows on the wooden table. Red shadow, blue shadow, green shadow, yellow shadow I held in my hand.

I didn't need the color shadows; I needed my Lion.

"No," the waitress said, "It's a very expensive and unique thing. It's also the chef's favorite thing and he bought it in Tokyo."

"So what?" I wanted to say, "And don't call my Red Lion "thing." The thing is you and probably, I'm not sure, me. But this Red Lion is He. He is not a thing; he is a sign."

I didn't say that. I didn't say so much important phrases in my life.

That lady, that waitress was so confident. She said as she cut in a Japanese blue silk dress with pink Sakura flowers, with perfect as a marble skin and slanting eyes she looked like Japanese deity or charming geisha and her words were as leaves: thin, steel, sharp. They cut my flesh, and she absorbed it.

"Have you been a Tokyo girl?" she asked.

I'm a Kyiv, not a Tokyo girl. But I would glad to be a Tokyo girl if I could get my Red Lion.

"No," I said.

"Oh," she said, "I can give you the address of the store where the chef bought this hashioki, and you can buy it while you're visiting Tokyo."

Oh, really? It's so easy.

Did I look like a person who was going to Tokyo next Monday?

Ok, maybe I would go there with the Next Ocean in my life.

On the other hand, it was a good sign. I believe we are 50% of what people think we are. I know, some people think I'm a bitch, a shark (that's my co-worker's thoughts); others think I'm just a cute girl, no more than 24 (ten years I'm no more than 24), nice, and of course, stupid.

That's why I am a deck chair the 50%, not 100%. I can give you a pleasure, but don't forget, I'm made from wood, I'm hard; use me with the sun and warmth and you'll enjoy me.

That night I knew two things: I won't see Tokyo this year (even if the waitress thought differently) and I wanted that Red Lion. So, how could I get it? Only one idea came to my head. I must show them how I mask and how important mask is for me.

I masked.

At the end of the dinner, when I had known that waitress was Umiko, and the chef's name was Yohei, and we hugged, Yohei told me, "If you come back, I'll probably give it to you."

Hm, probably, I thought, but I said, "Ok, I'll be back with my boyfriend, and I'll ask you to prepare your amazing corn for us."

"Ok," he said with Dionysius' smile. It entices, seduces, promises, and draws. "See you in two weeks."

I remember that day was the first Tuesday when I have been masking. I remember how my head ached. I remember, I was so nervous. I remember, I was in a white jeans, stripped vest and orange sneakers. The long purple Missoni headscarf was hugging my neck. I was alone and only a scarf could hug me. If you see me in a scarf, know that I'm lonely and it hugs me.

In two weeks, I came again. I was in a long white dress and my favorite silver shoes by Manolo Blahnik; I was with my boyfriend. If you see me in beautiful shoes, know that I'm not lonely and someone hugs me. My boyfriend prefers bright short dresses; I prefer long headscarves. That's how we live, that's how we love.

I was tired and wanted to drink. Umiko met us and led us to our table. They put Red Lion, my Red Lion, especially for me. I masked the candle and smiled. I put my palm on it; I made an eclipse; I closed my eyes and switch on the light.

I was so happy to mask again. I remembered they promised to give me my Red Lion if I would come back. But I didn't really believe them. Just because I mask and come back doesn't mean I will get what I want. Bitch or no bitch, shark or no shark. I'm just a cute girl, always no more than 24, nice, and of course, stupid.

We came to this restaurant just because our masks were masked, and because they had the best sushi in LA.

When we finished our dinner and all the guests had gone, Dionysius gave me a small silver bag. When we went outside, I opened the package and found my Red Lion.

Red Lion, my new mask means to me something very special, even magic. When I hold it in my hand; when I put it on my face, when I mask myself, I feel like I have the secret power. Mask is mine. Only mine. My Red Lion knows me, he golden powders me.

Mask is my symbol, my talisman; made from porcelain, so fragile, but I keep the mask with me every time when I need its power. Mask protects me, protects my deck chair, my Red Lion, my bitch, my shark, my stupid, stupid, very nice, very cute girl.

ANIMALS' LIFE

I returned from Polunin's concert disappointed. Of the three-hour performance, I suffered two. In two hours, Polunin only made two cameo appearances. He was on stage for a grand total of five minutes. It's ridiculous. For two hours I had to listen to some guy strumming his guitar (ok, his name is Estas Tonne and maybe someone knows him), who was playing weird, empty music, all the while brandishing an incense stick. Yes, you read that right, an Indian incense stick. He lit it at the beginning of his set and placed it at the head of his guitar. Every time one fizzled out, he set fire to another. Yes, when you're a terrible artist you have to create something to justify your shitty craft. The familiar spicy scent of all yoga studios mixed with the fumes of drunken Russian macho-men and their scented, dolled up Russian and Ukrainian tarts. There were no Americans or very few in the audience. The concert was in the heart of LA, but I felt like I landed in the heart of Moscow.

The doting audience resembled the cretin descendants of Jabba the Hutt: loud, smelly, with bright makeup, dressed to kill and satisfied with themselves. It's autumn in LA; it's as warm as a European summer. But ladies were dressed to the nines in magnificent fur coats, high boots, and felt hats. No one took off her apparel in the stinking, stuffy hall.

Anyone can spot a Russian abroad at first sight. And unfortunately, russian, and Ukrainian women still look very similar.

I felt ashamed that I was one of them. Maybe I don't look like them, but we do share common roots.

I wish I could be someone else. If I'm honest, I wasn't disappointed only in Polunin's concert.

I don't know who I really am. I tried to be someone I'm not. I loathe myself. I'm a fake, my own fake. I'm afraid of failure because I know, I can fail. I'm a failure. I don't believe in myself or in my own success, hence I pretend.

I pretend I'm strong; I pretend I know who I want to be; I pretend I'm in control my life; I pretend, I'm independent and all-sufficient, but I'm not. I pretend I love people; I pretend I love animals and kids; I pretend I love parents, but I don't. I pretend I'm brave and not selfish; I pretend I'm wise and intellectual; I pretend I have a good taste; I pretend I can forgive; I pretend I can accept; I pretend I can be a good friend; I pretend I can be a good wife. I pretend I want to be a wife. But I can't.

I can take care of my postmen. They scream and wait for my attention. I have to help them with their bank statement and boots with thick soles and sneakers, which are torn apart at the seams and cheap as Soviet laundry soap. They always smell of sweat and wait patiently, until they are fed and told a fairy tale. They want to believe that princes and princesses exist, and mice turn into fucking carriages, cars, flying ships, or whatever.

I'm telling you, this fucking life is a bitch and I'm her best friend. Do you know what I mean? Do you follow me? I mean I know how this world works. You are either on the top and fucking it, or it fucks you and doesn't ask if it hurts. Believe me, I know what I'm saying. When you are drunk you can eat and smell any shit and it will be sweet for you. Life is shit, so let's open this fucking bottle of two penny, magic Jim Beam; let's burn our withered throats like a glazier, turn the throats into Murano glass, a vase with colorful smooth lines and put flowers into it. I bought lilies. Five delicate buds cut and ready to die on my eyes, while I stand at the stove and fry bacon and eggs.

Bacon is one more dead body in my apartment, and I add to the dead pig unborn chicks. I love nature—I don't throw cigarette butts on the pavement, and I cry when I see someone mistreating a dog, but at the same time, I participate in this catena of death every day. Because of me and those like me, this pig and these chicks are slaughtered; because of me these lilies are cut, and I try not to think about it.

The flesh of a dead pig has darkened in a skillet. I do not like crispy bacon. I'm from Ukraine, I know what fat is; we call it "salo" and we eat it raw or, as we say, fresh. I grew up on fresh sausages, which were made today from a pig slaughtered in the morning. Yet yesterday that pig had the name Frosya and everybody loved her. So much love can kill you and you'll be eaten.

More rich families called their pigs Margot, and the goats were always Zor'ka, which means "dawn."

When I was seven, I came to my friend. She lived in a neighboring yard with her grandparents. It was summer morning; I wasn't at school. I opened the green gate (at the cemetery the gate is painted in blue), I was greeted with Rex, who was sitting on a chain and suddenly I saw the head of our beloved Zor'ka. It was impaled on a sharp fence post. Nearby hung her pink, still warm, recently fleeced skin.

We loved Zor'ka, we collected herbs for her and made her salads. Zor'ka was our friend. I don't know why grandparents decided to kill her with knitting needle. I still see her eyes on a severed head without skin and Rex waves his tail and looks on with love. Ripe mulberry lies on the floor, so my heels and Rex's ass are purple.

I still remember that day, how we cried; I still remember that day, how we refused to accept the death; I still remember that day, holding hands with my friend and us comforting each other; I still remember that day, our anger and our oath to always hate her grandfather. I still remember that day, that first time we wanted to take revenge, life for life.

GREEN DOOR

I hate cloudy mornings. I hate when everything around me has that sheen of dullness. I hate when dullness penetrates me, moves into my body, scrapes the sharp edges of my consciousness, and dulls the aches and pains that come from love.

I hate. I'm scared. I'm afraid I'll never see the sun. I'm scared everything around me will lose its color. I'm afraid that I am this dullness, this bleak coat of skin that covers the gloomy veneer of my heart.

I know I have to see him. It's now or never, that what he told me. When did he tell that? The time is the entangled chain with a cheap copper pendant in the pocket of a teenage girl who has been smoking, who just given her first blowjob and who is proud of herself and hates herself at the same time. Her nausea is the time's nausea, Sartre's nausea that sickens the sickness of the time, the sickness of the soul unable to face the time or the music. How does that song go? Face the music and dance.

I would dance if I could, but this dullness prevents me from even taking a step a turn into the dull world.

The time is knotty, but it rushes forward. It feels sick but it rushes forward. God, what am I doing here? Why did I come?
Yes, I'm brave. Yes, it's now or never. I'm brave, I'm proud of myself and hate myself at the same time. I'm not a teenager anymore, I'm a pendant. A cheap copper pendant in the pocket. "Stop it!" I said, "stop it!"

I stopped.

I stopped in front of his door.

The cloudy morning made everything grey. But his door, his door is always green. This entrance door as a green traffic light. It pushes me to put pressure on the gas. It pushes me to sweep with all speed. It pushes me to break all the rules. It pushes me. He pushes me. That's why I'm here.

I'm here, on this unknown street where I know every inch. Maple trees are unknown, but familiar as old friends, blue flowers are watching me. They froze and watch. I don't see their eyes, but I feel, they have them and they see better dogs, better owls, and even better cockroaches.

Sticky eyes.

They stuck to my orange sweatshirt and blue pants. They stuck to my strained nipples; they crawl over my brown hair. Like cockroaches, they creep into my mouth and look what I'm inside, what's there today.

They watch me, they see me, and they look through me, like he does.

And I'm scared, afraid.

The sun melts me as this white, flattened chewing gum on the grey asphalt. Someone spit it out—as he does, as he will spit me out.

I remember how he said, "I'll make you. I'll create you." We were in his room, his dark-blue room with the dark-brown wood table where he would create me, where he wanted to operate on me. His orange shirt smelled of fresh grass and wet earth. He was the earth, the ground after a summer rain. I was his rain. I was his storm. His stiff bristles scraped my tender cheeks. The lost or can be dropped from the rest, the silver drawing-pin was on the table. It reflected the yellow light of the room and our dark silhouettes. It could prick me, as he does. It could nail me to this wooden operating table as he did.

"No," I whispered. "You'll destroy me."

And now I'm here. Again. I'm standing in front of his green door; I'm standing in front of his green traffic light. With all my being I press on a nonexistent brake.

My orange sweatshirt and blue pants smell of fresh grass and wet earth. I'm the earth, the ground after a summer rain. He is my rain. He is my storm. He is my sun, which melts me as the white, flattened chewing gum on the grey asphalt.

I'm scared, I'm dullness.

He will destroy me.

It will create me.

I want it.

And I hate it.

I turn the door-handle.

SUPERMARKET

"Do you need a paper bag?" the cashier asked.

Such a stupid question. Pip, pip, pip, pip—the neighboring registers peep. The voices of sellers and buyers mingled and hang under the ceiling of the supermarket. A huge circular ceiling with metal beams. It resembles the ceiling of the airport, waiting room. We're waiting for the flights, here we're waiting for the calculation and line. I hate to wait. Time and thoughts seep through the waiting grid. Crawling. Like who? Who are you, girl in a green t-shirt with a piercing in the nose, and maybe in the tongue, who knows her?

Here are the smells of sweat, bread, vanilla biscuits, strawberry gum, and tangerines. I smell the gunpowder. There will be war. Soon there will be war. No! It's already here. There is always war: in the West, in the East; in the South, in the North; in the bed, in the head, between dogs, mice, humans, and cockroaches. Even between this saleswoman and me. She wants something from me. Something more.

Oh, I feel ice fires wake up through the storm. Frozen playful fire. Laughing, skipping shadows; they are the colors of the sunset, the colors of the moon. Will you marry me? But who needs you? But who needs me? Of course, I can understand everything. For God's sake, this is not anyone's news. What in general can be new in this world? Devotion? Love? Luck? What? We still don't know the difference between "unfaithfulness" and "betrayal." And if we know, who really feels it? I feel it. Oh Gods, what am I? Nothing new, and I and millions of others, and he's always amazed at something. We know nothing. We don't know everything. And in the desert the wind blows, the neighbors' dog barking in the yard with a raspy voice. And I smile when a girl of six years, touches this dog. Touches this bitch. I smile because this girl doesn't care what she knows and what she doesn't; she feels what she wants and just lives.

There is a black button on the floor here. Step on it or not? Maybe pick it up?

The cashier is drumming her fingers on the table. She's giving me that look. What do you want, bitch? I can touch you. Do you want to be my dog? Maybe you want to bark, gaff-gaff, gaff-gaff, gaff-gaff. In the desert, in which the wind blows, but doesn't carry anything alive; among the playful, cold tongues of fire, tongues of people. Hands smell of garlic. I cooked potatoes. Mom always, in the end, adds garlic, dill, and parsley. And at the very end, she sprinkles everything with black pepper. It was delicious. It was simple and delicious. And now? Hands smell of garlic and pepper tickles in the nose. I want to sneeze, but I can't. As an orgasm. I want to come, but I can't. Why can't I sneeze?

Heels hurt. I marked time. They always hurt when I trample a long time on the spot. When I'm running—my heels don't hurt. But when I'm marking time in this kitchen, when I'm vacuuming this living room—my heels hurt.

Here is the smell of black currant. Someone from the neighbors bakes a currant cake or they make jam. Gulls continuously squawk. A stupid voice, a stupid noise. There are people like gulls, with a gull voice too. That's not lucky. What luck do I have? Luck is very relative thing. When the leg was cut off, but didn't kill you, you stayed alive—was it lucky? Or when the husband left you for another woman and left you a house and a car, he pays the alimony and doesn't blow his nose when you smear a face with a night cream—is that lucky?

Dust on the bedside tables and on the floor. It's light, barely noticeable; thin, almost invisible; very young web in the upper right corner. There's one spider there. A lonely spider. A little spider sits or lies or stands and doesn't move. Maybe it died?

Lucky or unlucky, but we must live. Who and why must—it's not clear. That girl is six years old; she doesn't ask, she doesn't think, and she feels good. To hell with it, I'll take this bag.

"Yes, please," I said.

AGORA

There wasn't a cloud in the sky. It was one of those bright days, which makes one hazy with light, almost as if you were being interrogated by God for crimes you didn't commit. The sun spread its wings and embraced the whole sky, clasping it to its inner fire. People, like snakes, crept out of their shells and put their bodies under the sun; they warmed up their bones and set fire to their brains. The ocean heaved huge waves onto the shore, eroding the sand away. Surfers were sitting on their surfboards; mothers were smearing children's faces with sunscreen, fathers ate ice-cream and guzzled cans of beer; single women lay on towels, their swimsuits open, substituting their charms for the confident hands of the wind.

I went outside and sat on a bench before the horizon. The bright light hit me. I closed my eyes. There was too much light. I couldn't bear it. Like a knight in a metal helmet, I observed the beach and people through the narrow slots of my face.

"Too much light," I whispered to myself. "Too much light."

My inner darkness, my internal cloudiness shrank inside of me ready to burst into a thunderstorm like a heavy pregnant cloud. I put out a cigarette and went up to my room. I melted into the cool darkness of the apartment. I removed all my clothes and threw them to the floor. Therein lies some sort of pleasure—to throw clothes on the floor, it's like I'm shedding my old skin with all my unpleasant thoughts and mindless actions.

I'm naked, vulnerable. I have come to terms with my weakness. I tried to be strong permanently, but it broke me. I usually throw away broken things, even if they are not destroyed. It's easier to throw it away and buy a new one. It's rare that something is so valuable that I want to repair it.

Unfortunately, I'm too far away from being the kintsugi master. Unfortunately, I'm not a piece of pottery.

It's impossible to become clever without stupidity; to know the truth without agonizing doubts. Weakness equates itself to virtuous light, the power to the insidious darkness. Now I understand it, now I use it, now I feel it. And I feel my skin, still warm from the sun. My body is ready to become anew. I am ready to become anew again: a new woman, a new soul stirring up the old timid sand on the shore. I yearn to become new. Stroke golden scars and embrace the past as something to be proud of.

I crawled under the covers. My tightly closed eyes are like a jousting helmet, which better protects me from the all-pervading light. Today I don't need the light; today I hate the sun; today I surrender to my darkness.
I clenched; I turned into stone; I fell into a dream as if in a deep rocky gorge.

Images and thoughts mixed with the sounds of the waves and the noise of people—cars drove, children squealed, someone strummed the guitar, as another sang and clapped their hands. Images and thoughts morphed into the tunnels. The small stone rushed through them. Words from unwritten poems; pictures from unwritten novels; kisses from unknown men and women; touches of inaccessible surfaces, unworn clothes, unpurchased fabrics; tunes of forgotten, and unsung songs pulled me in different directions, cut me to pieces and made ribbons out of me, launching ribbons into the sky and sewing long dresses and skirts from them, weaving them into the hair of future characters, future children, future humans whose existence is dubious.

I woke up and started to clean my apartment. Only senseless chaos can be more meaningless than cleaning. When I finished, I went outside to my bench.

Sunday pass through me, and I through it—we dissolved into each other and with every minute we became the one past. The sun concealed itself. The pure blue color of the sky shifted to a bluish, purple, and gold. Even the mountains turned purple. The view reminded me of a self-decorated velvet-covered casket.
In the IV century, before the bloody victory of Christianity, Hypatia with her disciples observed the sunset. They sat on the steps of the

Royal Library of Alexandria and marveled at the sky. The same sky.

"What do you think is out there?" the first disciple asked.

"I don't know," the second disciple said.

"I know," the third one answered, "there's a cover. The lid of a huge casket in which we all sit."

Hypatia smiled.

"Then why is this lid one color in the afternoon, and another in the evening?" the first retorted indignantly.

"And where do these little shiny crumbs go in the morning?" the second asked.

"How do I know?" the third disciple barked. "The caskets are... different."

Hypatia smiled.

The sky looked at them in silence. The orange sun hid behind walls of high sand. The evening clouds slowly sailed by, and they were oblivious to the conversations of insignificant people on the steps of a large building. As obedient soldiers, they silently cruised along without understanding where and why.

It was 391 A.D., half a century after the Council of Nicea and the creed that shaped the boundaries of Christianity for years to come.

A few years after this day, Christians would destroy the temple of Serapeum and plunder the Library of Alexandria. A few more years later, Hypatia would become the first human to discover that the Earth revolves around the Sun, only than to be declared a witch.

In 415 Davus, her former servant and secret admirer, would strangle her so that she wouldn't suffer at the hands of the new Christians, the monks of parabalani, who stoned her naked body lying in the street. At least, Alejandro Amenábar and Mateo Gil think like this.

1604 years passed, and I'm still sitting in the huge casket full of treasures and stones, not understanding, hesitant to label myself as either treasure that is worth being repaired or a stone, that should be thrown away. Meanwhile, the Earth revolves around the Sun, and every minute we become part of the past beating savagely against the future.

Hypatia smiles.

WALLS

Thoughts morphed into a dark chocolate.

Sweet and bitter, they're melted by my body's warmth, flowing down my temples, cheeks, trickling on to the lips, before finally moistening my mouth. I feel their chocolaty taste, licking it on the tip of the tongue, waving across the palate and sky, I swallow. Chocolaty thoughts stream down my chin, crawl to the collarbone and ensconce, like a latex, my neck.

I went to the blue wall and stopped.

The wall overgrows with trees. What kind of the trees is it? Their rough fronds reaching for my wrists, they always reach for my wrists. What kind of the trees does always reach for my wrists? In the dark forest I saw a thousand different trees. I didn't know their names. I don't know their names and their types. I only know they want me. They emerge from the darkness of my forest, unexpectedly. They are waiting for me to give up; when I relax and let my owls go for a walk; give them my eyes and they tie my thoughts to their roots.

Under my feet wet, yellow, fallen leaves. Fallen leaves of this year lie on the fallen leaves of the past year. Layers. Leaves lie on the leaves. The new covers the old. Layers. I stand on many layers. They crunch—old, new, rotten, fresh layers. I trample them. Autumn gets into my mouth with dampness, autumn lives in my nose, I always smell the smell of fall.

Two sparrows. One crow. They are sitting upstairs, while a dead, wingless seagull lies below. These birds have teeth, it should be noted. My silver dress reflects their red insidious eyes. The smell of the rain and wet asphalt, the smell of wet black soil emanates from the wall.

A small cross, given to me by my parents for my sixteenth birthday, cuts into my right palm. I squeezed it tightly. From the beginning, when I just arrived. I have long wanted to come here. My brown hair is an extension of brown branches. We merge, long merge, long together. Previously, she came at night and stroked my hair. It was necessary for her, it was necessary for my hair. Now that my thoughts have turned to chocolate and I can eat and drink them, truth to tell, if I drink them, I need to dilute them with water, but it's better with milk, fresh, warm, which still smells of the mother's womb, even if the mother is a cow or a goat, let her be a cow or a goat instead a pig or a dog; now with chocolate thoughts I can understand everything that I did not understand and rejected before.

I wish to recline on this green sofa. It rode to me on its wooden, curly legs. Bad legs. Beautiful, but bad. I repeatedly stub my pinky toes, against them, first the right, then the left. Poor little toes. I torment them so much. I smack them against the sharp hard corners; I torture them with narrow, cramped shoes; I wear heels for my own pleasure, but the little toes despise them.

I opened my palm.

The cross fell to the floor. Golden, small, with the golden crucified Jesus lying on the floor. I don't want to trample him, but I'm aware that I can. I can do it completely by accident. I know because I would never dare do such things; I don't do them on purpose. Poor Jesus. Although he is gold, he is still poor.

I touch the wall, it is as soft as blue moss, velvet; I feel its lively playful villi. My fingers fall into the wall. She said all the walls are soft. She said the walls are nonexistent, and those that are, those are soft, so these are not the walls. Everything makes sense when you accept the notion that the walls are soft and porous; then the walls do not exist, then everything changes. And with chocolate thoughts, which are smeared all over the body, to pass through the walls is delicious. It is good when it's delicious. Everything changes when it's delicious. It's very important not to lose taste if you know what I mean. Do you follow me? Without taste, you will never understand what is tasty and what is disgusting. I know what I'm saying. Believe me, I'm dying if I'm lying.

I wiped the corners of my mouth with my right index finger. They had a lot of chocolate. Liquid and dust like corners. I'm telling you, silent, gloomy people love corners too. I always put a chair in the corners. But today I am a visitor. It's indecent to move furniture while you're visiting. Let it move by itself, as it pleases.

I put my right arm into the wall, up to my elbow. Well done, you. When you pass through the walls, the ceiling suddenly disappears. It does so on its own, without even needing to ask. She let me touch the cotton and said that the clouds were even softer. What could be softer than cotton wool? Maybe the wool of a fluffy cat. But cats are completely unrelated to heaven.

Jesus should have soft skin and fluffy hair; he was born amongst the goatlings. Perhaps, among the sheep and donkeys also. As long as it's not among pigs and dogs.

It's time for me to go to the blue wall. It's time for the ceilings to disappear.

PUPPY

"Don't do this," she says, "I beg of you."

His right palm is clenched into a fist. His unshaved chin juts forward. Two buttons on his crimson polo were unbuttoned. He resembles a beast. Her skin observes his power yet at the same time, is well aware his power is also his biggest weakness. Dry air tickles her nostrils. She's cold. Her frightened skin shivers under the blue blouse. She remembers what he did the last time. She suffers from the effects of his selfish actions every day. She knows, she will go through this, but she doesn't want this. The white walls close in on her. What was once a huge room, now shrinks into a small box. She feels trapped inside this shabby and crushed pack of cigarettes which lies on the grey concrete floor. He slowly blinked.

He feels his red polo is suffocating him from breathing. He wants to rip it off. He wants to breathe freely. Dry air, like ice water, doesn't quench his thirst. The more he ingests this air, the more he wants it. Unlike her, he always wants more. He loves her intensely, but concurrently, he hates this love. He hates that he needs her around him and doesn't understand, why he needs her exactly. He feels tension on his sticky, sweaty back. Her words, her supplications always sound like complaints. "She provokes me." He wants to yell but he knows, he can't do that. Right now, he doesn't understand why he loved her, chose her. Why this strange woman is living with him over the last nine years. Here is stuffy and dark, but he sees white walls. He sees how they dissolve and turn into a white, dense rubber. He feels his power. He feels that he can take and destroy everything around him as easy as stepping on and crushing this shabby pack of cigarettes on the brown wooden floor. He feels his power, but at the same time, he's afraid that she could become stronger than he. And just as he comes to this realization, he becomes weak. He opens his hand.

The smell of cattle and livestock fills their throats. It seems the hall is full of horses and cows. He loves this aroma; she hates this putrid smell. He wears these smells all day into the evening, whereupon she pleads with him to take a shower before he even steps over the threshold of their home. His home. He lost his home, his private space and sanctuary for his thoughts. The bright light from the soffits overhead dazzles her. This light is his sun, his assistant. This bright light exposes everything around him. He wishes he could harness the same light at home. But their home is her territory. He doesn't need all that furniture, curtains, new wallpapers that she changes every three years and things, which make his house look like an artificial picture from a magazine. Of course, an artificial house doesn't have space for real life, for wildlife, for natural life. All his life he felt that he was at one of nature. He was always sure of who he was, who he would be.

"Tom, please," she says, "don't look at me like this. Don't do it."

He sees her wet lips and a small mole on the left chin. He remembers, on their first date, he thought this birthmark was a speck of dust and he tried to wipe it off with a damp napkin. It was funny. They laughed. When was the time they shared a laugh together? His memory fails him.

"Tom, I'm tired," she says. "You turned our house into a manger. Five pets, Tom. Five! Their fur is everywhere! I can't breathe; it's in my scrambled eggs and sandwich; it's all over my clothes. Tom, I don't understand you. You work with animals, why can't you just leave them at your job? Why must I live in a zoo? I want to live in a cozy, clean house!" she yells.

He catches his breath. He takes her hand. "Look," he says, "look at his eyes."

She knows it's a trap. She knows if she does this, he'll win, again.

"Please, Tom," she whispers, "don't do that."

A small, sad mongrel looks out from its cage with two small, beady eyes, filled with sadness. Its curly long hair sticks out in all directions. It has a black spot on its chin.
"Do you take this puppy?" a volunteer asks.

FAULT

"Look what you've done," he whispered.

The night lights of the city break into the room as pilferers and peeping toms; they don't loot jewelry; they neither pillage nor plunder, but they intrude upon the intimate enclosure of a small sleeping apartment; as pilferers and peeping toms, they leave marks on the dusty floor and the high carpet, replete with spiky crumbs of stale bread and damp chips; their sticky palms, as palms of strangers, leave their mark on the furniture; their ugly mouths fog the mirror, leaving a wet spot that invites the finger to write "I was here. I was not here."

The din of the street beats on the tightly closed windows; like a night moth flapping its wings, it retreats and batters its target with renewed vigor; the scream fights back defiantly, only to be defeated; it burned its feathers and crashed to the ground, crashed to the same floor with spiny crumbs of stale bread and damp chips.

Her breath intertwined with his pulse, like an inner elusive impulse of movement, it pushed him to follow her, to go, to flock, to pursue, to hunt, to drive, to strive, to desire, to mix thoughts, to mix tears, to mix blood, to mix lives. Her cheeks are still wet with tears; they're hot, red, and wet, sticky like the palms of pilferers and prying gaze of peeping toms. They tremble, there is blood on them, blood on his hands, blood on the gray wall, blood on the wooden dusty floor and high carpet; there is blood on his Levi's blue t-shirt, there is blood on her yellow ZARA dress. She stopped breathing. When did she stop breathing?

He took her by the shoulders and hoisted her up. Her head was like a heavy bud, a heavy bud of the red velvet rose; a wormy, wormy rose on a thin early ripening of a bud stem, leaned back. He stood, as a knight at initiation, on one knee. There was a crushed cigarette under his knee. He didn't notice it, he didn't feel it, he doesn't feel it. How couldn't he feel the crunch of Barry's broken neck, his little hamster, Barry. Barry just stopped breathing, like her, he suddenly stopped breathing. But even though lifeless, Barry was his Barry. Yes, he became stiff, yes, he no longer ate and ran around the cage; yes, he began to emit a foul odor, but it was still his Barry, the same beloved Barry.

"You are no longer cheerful," he said while stroking the motionless Barry, who was starting to decompose. "But I still love you, I love you the way you are. You don't need to be playful and good all the time; I love you; you don't need to be kind for me to love you. You can do nothing, just as now, you can just lie down and sleep, my lovely Barry, sleep".

Mom scolded me a lot. But I'm not to blame, I didn't want that. I loved Barry, I wasn't to blame," he whispered to her body.

Her pink warm lips, in the morning they smiled, in the morning he heard their laughter, he looked inside them; looked at that resilient pink tongue with young white teeth. She hid everything in pink. Even between her legs, she hid a pink color, the pink color hid between her vertical nude lips. Her smooth bosom crowned her white torso and flowed down to her hairless pubic area; forever a virgin, forever clean, even now with streams of viscous blood and his creamy cum, she hasn't lost her pink color; she's still clean and no one will pollute her.

What have you done?" someone whispered. "What have you done?"

He turned his head. He tried to find who was waiting for his answer. He dropped her bud, he dropped her pink color and pressed himself to the window. The night lights of the city squeezed his neck; the noise of the street beat on his eardrums; Barry scented her dark blood, he smelled her blond hair, he took a spiny crumb of stale bread from her cheek. Shadows dance on the walls and glided on the floor; colored lights, red, blue and white replaced each other; helicopter blades are beating the night sky and a white spotlight is sliding on the window, sliding on the still black and white curtains. Everything here is frozen in death; only Barry came back to life, he's tossing again and moving his pink nose and a long mustache.

I'm not guilty, I didn't want that," he yelled. "Mom don't beat me, I'm not guilty, I didn't want that! I don't, mama, I don't!"

EMPTINESS

I closed the door.

He stayed with his suitcases on the staircase. He was waiting for the elevator. He flew away again. With him, in those two grey Rimova suitcases—his whole life. And I remained here. In this empty apartment on Ivana Franko Street with my whole life.

His skin was saturated with the aroma of Montale Aoud Lime. The sweet scent of his body, his unique scent, which I recognized from thousands of others, mixed with this perfume. His scent soaked the walls of this apartment, the sheets on which we slept, ate, loved, read; he soaked the parquet floor, bathroom tile and towels, long curtains in the rooms, pages of books on the shelves, clothes in the closet, my underwear in the top drawer of the dresser, dishes, cutlery in the kitchen, the red tablecloth on the roundtable, leaves of the Ficus tree and orchids on the windowsill in the living room, my written notebooks on my work desk; he soaked my hair, my skin, my bones, my blood, my thoughts. His smell runs through my veins. When I sense his aroma, I understand, that is how my heart smells.

I turned the latch on the door and saw her. I saw Emptiness. Again. She was standing beside the shelves with books and porcelain statues of houses that we brought with him from our joint travels. We didn't buy the very first house; it was given to us in business class when we flew from Amsterdam to Seoul. White, with blue windows and doors. Thereat we were glad that we flew together and would bring two houses home at once. And now he is gone, and her thin, long gray fingers without nails, are touching our houses, touching the blue windows and doors. Fingers without nails, mouth without teeth and tongue, eyes without pupils, only marsh-colored whites. Her pale body, covered with sticky mucus, is her dress; a black hole on her face is her mouth; she stands silently; she leaves her sticky mucus everywhere, she moves her fingers about, as though they were jelly threads, and looks at me.

"Quit it!" I said. She stopped, but she didn't answer. She sat down on the green sofa and folded her arms on her bony gray knees. The pack of Captain Black cherry cigarettes and a yellow lighter lie on the coffee table, in front of the sofa. We loved to smoke on our little balcony. From there, you can see the orange roofs of old houses and glass high skyscrapers; you can see our quiet street, along which cars rarely pass; you can see a neighboring house where a mongrel dog always barks from the second floor.

Two empty glasses, with traces of our lips and the remains of Riesling Auslese are on the table. They're waiting for me to take them to the sink. His guitar lies in the next chair. The guitar looks at me reproachfully. He was singing:
Always somewhere
I'll back to love you again
Miss you where I've been
I'll back to love you again

And now his guitar is silent and looks at me with conviction, as if it was my fault that he had left, as if it was my fault that he no longer sings, and it is silent now.

"What do you need from me?" I said to the guitar. "Why are you looking at me like that? What can I do?"

The guitar, defiantly, fell into her place in the corner near the window. Emptiness remained sitting on the couch. I burst into tears and sat down beside her. His white T-shirt lay on the back of the couch. I took it and inhaled the scent, inhaled the scent of my heart. I decided to put it on, but I was embarrassed by these vile silent pupils of Emptiness.

I went to the bedroom, in the hope that this creature would remain sitting on the couch. I didn't want her to see me naked. It was enough that she saw me as weak. But she followed me.

Since then, she has been following me all the time. She sits at the table in the kitchen, when I beat eggs for an omelet, she walks next to me in a supermarket, watches as I put products in a basket, as I look for the date on the package with yogurt and butter, as I make a choice of a soft avocado and hard green apples; she stands next to me when I take a shower, lather my hair with shampoo, shave my legs, brush my teeth, smear my face with day cream; she sits next to me on the subway, goes with me on the stairway, walks with me to the toilet. She sits down next to me when I meet friends and if I laugh, if I forget about her for a moment, stop seeing her for a moment, stop feeling her for a moment, she puts her cold fingers on my neck and smothers me, slowly. She doesn't break me and my bones; she crushes me, squeezes my neck, chest, temples—such is her heavy price for distraction.

I don't know if it was his plan. Maybe he has an old arrangement with her, and she must be with me every time he departs. I don't know if she will be here if he doesn't come back. Again. Is she here only because he promised to come in a month? Is she here because he told her to watch over me? Why didn't he ask me if I want to live with her? I told her to leave, but she doesn't respond to me. I see in her eyes without pupils that she hears me. I see her toothless mouth moving, but she is silent, she doesn't answer. Silent, she does as she sees fit.

I tried to seduce her. We lay together in my and his bed. She lay on his side. I hugged her. She didn't push me away; she didn't answer. My pink lips came close to her pale lips. I kissed her. At first, only on the lips. She didn't push me away; she didn't answer. I put my tongue in her mouth. That's how I learned she has no tongue. There is a vague yet palpable vacuousness in her mouth. Absolute abyss. I felt nauseous. I barfed on her, on his pillow, on our purple sheets with red stripes, on my white silk nightgown.

I didn't touch her anymore.

Yesterday, I wrote to him, "Please take your Emptiness with you."

He didn't answer.

MY FATHER'S DAUGHTER

I was in 9th grade when my father told me, "Natasha, we need to talk."

It was unexpected. I remember my father as an introverted, very calm person. Usually, we didn't have a kind of "father and daughter" conversations. I only heard that it was a time when my dad was a bright active man, who was a great football player and a budding political prospect with endless possibilities. He was young, smart, and confident. The whole Soviet world was open to him, and he was open to it. They admire each other. Then, suddenly—for people like my parents it was sudden—reformation (or dissolution) began. I was a child of reformation; I am a child of dissolution. When the Soviet Union crashed, my father, as a confident person, crashed too. And I hadn't a chance to see who he was, just who he became.

That evening we were sitting in the kitchen. I just finished washing the dishes—my parents never had a dishwasher—and made us some black tea. It was a quiet spring evening. The small wooden window was ajar. Sleepy flies and active mosquitoes were beating against the mesh stretched in a frame. A streetlight burned in the street. Its white light, which more illuminated the immediate area around itself than the courtyard pavement penetrated our third-floor apartment. Shone as the wailing call of an urban lighthouse. Our apartment sat on the same level as the bulb of the streetlight, which meant we were one of the lucky few that basked in its dim glory.

Sometimes at night, when I was doing homework until the morning, I would come to the kitchen and not turn on the light, prepare myself instant coffee with condensed milk. I was 14 years old. I didn't know the taste of espresso; I didn't know the words "latte and cappuccino." There was only Nescafe Gold in our house and in the kiosk, we could buy McCoffee 3-in-1: a sweet, watery, sandy, coffee-colored liquid. It's beyond me, that in the Ukraine, even now, 16 years later many people still drink Nescafe Gold, McCoffee and know nothing of espressos, lattes, and cappuccinos.

I spent many nights sitting in silence in my parents' kitchen, sipping instant coffee under the pale light of this curious lantern. It was like my silent suitor. He didn't need anything, but to see me and sit beside me.

That evening, my silent suitor was with me and my dad. The kitchen lamps were switched on, but I still felt his presence.

I sat down in front of my dad.

I was nervous. I couldn't remember the last time my dad told me something like that. Had he ever said anything like that to me? When a person says, "we need to talk" it generally means they need to say something to you. He or she, not the both of you—this "We" and "Us." How many of the thoughts, opinions, and feelings of others have been hidden and forced into these pronouns.

With my palm, I felt a sticky stain on a white enamel tablecloth. Mom will be angry that I've wiped the table badly, I thought. A crumpled napkin and crumbs of white bread lay in a transparent plastic breadbasket. In the crystal vase were candies—Karakum, Daisy, and Red Poppy. My mother adores sweets. She showed me how to add condensed milk to coffee. If she had her way, she would add condensed milk to everything. I've never had a sweet tooth and I still don't have one now, but coffee with condensed milk and strawberries with condensed milk are still my favorite food pairing.

Next to the vase was a matchbox. It reminded me that before going to sleep, I must not forget to shut off the gas on the stove. Mom always demanded to shut it off. At the same time, every night before going to bed, she went and checked whether the gas was turned off or not. If not, she became upset and scolded me, my dad, and my brother for forgetting to turn off. "What for?" I said. "You'll do it yourself anyway. So, why should we do it?" Such rebellious banter was a big no-no in my family. Usually, anything Mom said was the law, and failure to comply would generally bring grave punishment along with it. Mom was the dictator. Dad was sheepish, silent companion. And now they switched roles and Mom lie silently in the bedroom, watching Poirot for the fifth, no, the tenth time. And now it was Dad's turn to take on the mantle of authoritarian.

"Ok," I said, "what do you want to talk about?"

Maybe he wants to give me a long lecture about safe sex and remind me, or himself, that I'm a young woman and an unwanted pregnancy is an unwanted pregnancy; in other words, you are young, and we don't want to be grandparents. No one ever talked to me about it, neither Mom nor Dad. Probably, they think I'm still too little for those types of conversations. But to be honest, half of my class are no longer virgins. Some lost it in the 6th grade and the others last year. I'm surprised no one's gotten pregnant yet. Probably, they are waiting for graduation. Maybe now my father thinks the time has come. Maybe he thinks that his words can help me to be safe, or they will help him to think that he will be safe, and he did all that he could and my problems at the future will be only mine.

Or does he want to say that he won't be able to pay for my studies and I need to stay till to 11th grade and then apply for a scholarship? But I had already chosen a university and it was cheaper than Odessa Legal Academy.

Or maybe he anticipates that I'll pester him to let me go to the disco? But Mother doesn't let me go, so I don't see the point in such a chat. Besides, he had never been interested in such questions before. Generally, after I turned 8, he wasn't interested in what was happening in my life at all.

Fuck, what if someone told him that I kissed Pasha, from the neighbor's yard? My parents mentally have already married me with Dima, whom I have been dating for the last two years. My mom loves Dima. What my father thinks about him I have no idea. But recently, my relationship with Dima entered a new phase in which I tried to break up with him and he tried to save our young sinking ship. I didn't tell my parents about it. For them, Dima is a sweetheart and we're the perfect couple. Our mothers were discussing already where and how we would get married and what kind of meat and fish would be served at the wedding reception. We're only 14 and 15 And I'm still a virgin. Yes, we're like Romeo and Juliet, but everyone remembers how love ends at this age. You either die physically or psychologically, it doesn't matter. The main thing is you will die earlier than you should. Oh, I wish I could read thoughts. How much easier this world would be.

All these thoughts buzzed and circled in my head like flies and bees over freshly sliced watermelon. My father was 54 years old. He was still, what we call, young and beautiful. When I think about that evening now, 16 years later, I think, "God, he was such a hot man!"

I remember the first time when I realized—for me it was sudden—that my father was an elderly man. It happened on his 68th birthday. Those two numbers, in that particular arrangement, made me cry the whole day.

My mother always said, "Even when you are 90, for us you'll always be a child." I think all good parents think and feel like this. And we, good children, always think that our parents will be forever young, forever 30 and 40, forever full of energy, forever wise and smart, forever strong and independent. It's such bullshit that people don't change. Everything changes. Changes come in that specific moment when you least expect them. And we can do nothing but accept that fate. That's it.

My father's head was almost gray. The skin on his hands was rough; his fingers became a little less mobile than usual. His face wore noble wrinkles. They were not the wrinkles borne from old age, they were from a life fully lived, much like ripened grapes, which absorbed the oppressive heat of the sun and now begin to shrivel by condensing sugar under the skin.

"You're a young woman," my father said, "and you live in a man's world."

"Ok," I said.

His words sounded peculiar. If I didn't know my dad, I would've thought that he listened to Nina Simone and that she inspired him. But I knew my dad never listened to any music. Ever. Even now I can't fathom how he could live without music in his life. Was there for him some sort of substitute?

"You have to remember," he said, "many times in this life there will be a choice between you and a man. And each time, most people will choose the man."

"What?" I thought. "Why?" I said.

I couldn't understand what he meant.

"Because you're a woman," he said, taking a deep breath.

It seemed like an invisible load was piled on his shoulders; like a mountain of brown bags of sand or flour set atop on his shoulders. He was weary. Like the words sucked the power out of him. As if the more he spoke, the heavier the bags on his shoulders. A white t-shirt, which just a few minutes ago had fit a slender frame with a gray, hairy chest, now hung on the hunched shoulders of a tired man.

"Because. . ."

I saw how he fumbled, trying to find the right words.

"Because usually, people think that men are better than women. You have to remember; they will always prefer men. You," the words broke like a string on a guitar, "if you want to achieve something in this life, you must be better than any man. You must always fight."

"Ok," I said just not to be silent.

My dad went to the bedroom. I heard the creak of the bed when he lay down on his side of the bed. He and my mom never changed the sides of the bed. Never.

I stayed in the kitchen with the lantern and the spring outside the window. I took a rag and wiped the table again. I turned off the gas. I turned off the light. I fight.

MY MOTHER'S DAUGHTER

When I was 8, my mom told me, "Never be addicted to a man."

We were in the kitchen. I was peeling potatoes; my mother was cooking borsch. It was a Saturday morning. Dad was in the bedroom watching football. It was sunny day. "Girl, you'll be a woman soon" played on the radio. I didn't know English well. My knowledge was only enough to say, "Kyiv is the capital of Ukraine and I'm on duty today."

But that song I understood not with my mind, but with something deep inside of me. It's as if I could read and understand with my skin and ears if they were so capable. I was humming the melody of this song. At the same time, I felt I had to answer my mom; however, I didn't know how to respond. Mother always needs an answer—that's what I used to think. It took me many years to untangle my delusions. In that specific moment, I couldn't dig up an answer and so I decided to pretend I didn't hear her.

I threw the peeled potato into the metal orange bowl and fetched a new one. For me that potato was new, but for itself, it was aged. Its brown skin was wrinkled and covered in fine folds. The potato was soft, still elastic, but not as firm as in its youth. The knife with which I peeled it dug into its flesh and got stuck.

"Mummy, can I take another knife?" I said.

"What's wrong with that one?" she asked, not looking at me.

I sat at the table. Mom stood with her back to me at the table near the stove. While I was peeling potatoes, she managed to form cutlets from minced meat and fry them in a griddle (the sweet smell of roasted meat spread throughout the apartment, it aroused hunger and whetted an appetite), grated the carrots and cut the onion. She never cried when she sliced onions. She didn't cry then, during my childhood years, and still doesn't cry to this day. I, on the contrary, roared then and continue to roar now. I still can't understand—does she make it a conscious habit to hold back her tears, or does she hail from the land of immortals where they're all immune? Tears in our family were unwelcomed, if not banned. If you had to cry, cry so that no one saw you; but it was better not to cry at all, even from an onion, even when your heart and soul yelled and pleaded for help. How many unshed tears does my mother keep bottled up within her?

"It's blunt," I said, "I can't peel this potato with it." Instantly, I bit my tongue.

What have I done, I thought. To my eyes, my mother's eyes flashed with the demonic fire that descends upon the eyes of women who gleefully anticipate the hour of reckoning. Mom's chin went up as mine simultaneously dropped. If it could, if I could, I together with my chin would fall through the ground, or at least to the second floor, to the neighbor below us. Mom wiped her hands, soaked in onion juice, on her checkered red apron. She went to the drawer and took out another knife. She brandished it in her right hand and with her thumb pressed down on the blade. Isn't she afraid of cutting herself, I thought?

"Mom, doesn't it hurt?" I asked.

"These knives can only strangle cats," she bristled.

My mom has a great sense of humor. Thanks to it, I could recount many catchphrases taken strength from Soviet films along with their figurative meaning.

"And your dad doesn't care," she said.

She always emphasized "your dad" as if to say I consciously chose my father, and it was my fault, and so henceforth I'm forever at fault and must bear responsibility for his actions; offer myself as the perpetual scapegoat. I didn't understand what exactly I owed, I merely understood I owed, that's it.

"He doesn't spend the whole day in the kitchen," she continued and then she yelled "Lesha, sharpen the knives!"

I knew, if Mom called my dad "Lesha", with a strong accent on the first syllable, so that the second syllable was practically not pronounced, it hissed "shhhhhaaa". It meant she was angry, but not very much, and she could comport herself and still be nice. When Mom is very angry, she calls Dad by his full name—Alexey.

Father didn't answer. Perhaps he just didn't hear her. Or maybe he just didn't want to—didn't want to answer or didn't want to hear.

"Alexey!"

Mom called even louder.

"Yes," Father said from his room.

"Sharpen the knives!"

I heard the unmistakable sound of sizzling meat; as the red-hot frying pan together with the fat, tortures it, smolders the flesh, killing every last living thing remaining on the inside. My little kid feet were bolted to the floor, I felt unable to move. I'm not sure if I just couldn't or wouldn't. It's seemed to me that if I didn't make any sudden moves, I wouldn't exist, and I would go unnoticed. I felt very sorry for my father. However, I felt sorry for my mother at the same time. Why are they together if they hate to speak to each other so much?

I don't know why but in this simple everyday situation, my thoughts sauntered toward feelings of hatred. I'm not even sure why I recalled this entire experience. The experience of the moment in which a husband and wife, two loving people, are oblivious to each other, unable to even hear the other, refusing to understand and help each other.

I hated that old potato. I hated myself. Why didn't I keep silent? I could've kept peeling with that blunt, bladeless knife. Yes, I would've been uncomfortable; but I could suffer, I had to suffer if only so my mother wouldn't be angry with my father, and my father wouldn't be so cold and indifferent with my mom.

Many years, while I was living with my parents, my mother repeated over and over to me "Never be addicted to a man."

I've never asked her why. I thought it would be wrong to pose that question to her, giving the impression that I didn't understand her; but I did. I understood her then and I understand her now.

I'm aware that being a mother is a very difficult, oft thankless job; you always feel inadequate. All good parents feel it; all good people feel it. We have only to accept it.

When I called up my wedding, when I said "no" to my first possible suitor, my mother was the first person who couldn't comprehend why I did that. She didn't support my decision.

"Why won't you get marry him? He's such a good catch!" she said.

Yes, he was, but I didn't want to be addicted to him. I didn't feel we would be happy.

I grew up in two realities: my parents and my own. They didn't fight a lot, but at the same time, I've never seen them madly in love with each other either. I mean, the clichéd type of love Hollywood regurgitates over and over ad nauseam. I've never seen them happy. If they weren't happy together, why did they get married—for tasty borsch and sharp knives?

I interrogated my parents: "Why didn't you divorce, or at least, why didn't you, Mom, leave Dad for another man; or you, Dad, why didn't you get a mistress?"

"We lived for you, our kids," they said.
Did they really live FOR us? It seems they didn't live BECAUSE of us, their children. I now know how I don't want to live my life, but I'm still perplexed as to how I want to live it. I'm my mother's daughter; yet still I don't know it.

FAREWELL

Somehow too many endings.

I'm leaving Los Angeles; I'm leaving new friends; I'm leaving Santa Monica beach; I'm leaving warmth and sunshine; I'm leaving eternal summer; I'm leaving a writing course.

Tomorrow, I'm leaving my lover. Probably, maybe, perhaps, possibly, perchance, potentially, on the cards I'm leaving the best man in my life; I'm leaving myself, some part of me. Which one? We'll see.

I listened to Pugacheva and cried. Pugacheva. Pugacheva! God, it's a sign. No, it's a clue that I'm either depressed or too old and ready to die. But I'm only thirty. Yes, I am smiling woman, and like the cat, I have nine times to die. I'm not sure what number it is. I stopped to count; I don't remember when I stopped to count. I keep only the total amount.

I have nine times to die, I'm like the cat, I lay on the beach, the famous Californian beach, which offers itself as some poetic allegory for Heaven. Can I say I'm thirty and I'm in Heaven? Can I? No, I'm still alive. I lay motionless, without music, silent. A fluffy blue towel is beneath me. It smells like "sunny morning" at least that's what the manufacturers call the fragrance. I'm in a blue swimsuit, blue sky above me, and the blue ocean crashing ashore from my left side. I didn't choose this blue range. It just happened. Maybe it chose me?

I'm thirty; I'm not in Heaven; everything is blue. I'm blue.

Thoughts fly by like a subway train while I sit on a wooden bench, at the station, and casually watching the wagons come and go. I don't embark. I sit motionless, silent, and blue.

The waves in this blue ocean come and go. My hours in this life come and go. I don't embark; I'm motionless and silent.

Somehow it is difficult and pleasurable for me at the same time. I wonder, does the caterpillar hurt when it morphs into a butterfly? To me it seems so; yes, it hurts. It hurts because any transformation process is painful. To experience pain during transformation is unavoidable. Isn't it?

The sun is baking my left side. Very warm, hot even.

I feel like I'm shading my old skin. The outer layer easily disappears; I emerge from it as from out of a dried, fragile womb. Cocoon. Cocoon? No, this word doesn't register. It's not a cocoon; it's a womb, bubble. Yes, it's a bubble!

I remember a few months ago, in a dance therapy class, I felt a bubble around me. It was outside, and I was inside. It protected me. "Why do I need a protective film around me?" I thought. But I enjoyed the warm embrace of that protective bubble.

Limbo.

The bubble burst.

When the bubbles burst, they stick to the skin. You need to clean yourself of their sticky residue. Rip it off.

Hubba Bubba chewing gum.

As a child, I blew big pink bubbles. They burst and stuck to my face; they had to be torn off from the cheeks, nose, chin, ears, eyebrows, and neck. It was especially difficult to clean the hair. The sweet pink remnants stuck and held my hair with all their rubbery strength.

This is exactly what I feel now: the inflatable bubble burst; the sticky shell covers my whole body; in some areas it pulls of easily, like Hubba Bubba from the cheeks, and in other places it clings to the skin, seeking to become one; it tugs the hairs on the skin, these thin, soft hairs on my skin; and in yet other areas, it seems to be stoke permanently; it keeps tight hold of me.
The process is unpleasant, but I am glad that the bubble burst. Only one thought scares me—what if Dante was right?

I'm thinking about the bubble, limbo, and Hubba Bubba instead of thinking thoughts of farewell. I can't compose the right farewell letters. I can't even have the right farewell thoughts. Maybe I can't say goodbye? Farewell. It should be gentle, romantic, subtle, stilted and deep.

But, let's be honest. There is no romance in goodbyes and farewells. There is a vile feeling of hopelessness, inability to change, to do what I want, and not how it turns out and nor should be.

Emptiness is inside me; agony and crumpled pieces of reality hover like space debris in the black abyss of chaos inside me. The moment, no matter how I try, doesn't linger; it rushes through me, at me, inside me and crumples. Crumples. I see this sand now, I hear these powerful, absolutely beautiful waves, but no matter what I wrote about them, no matter how hard I try to peer at them, look at them and remember them, everything is in vain; the brain crumples it.

iCloud offers a choice: store photos in there an original size or to optimize space by compressing them. I could press the button and permanently lose the full resolution of these photos; watch as small squares devoid of clarity naturally blur when magnified, smear the nuances, look and think "Oh, I remember that day, yes, it was good then," but it's not for me. I always choose "save in original size." I need the real size. I need the fullness of reality.

My brain doesn't offer me a choice. It works automatically. I want to exclaim and say, "What the hell? I'm the boss! This is my device! I do what I want!" And then I face the harsh reality that I, much like all of humanity, am allowed to survive only for one reason—I'm not in control of anything including my own body. We don't get to control. Everything has already been predetermined. And thank God, because I think I wouldn't last a minute if I got full control over my body. To breathe, to contract hundreds of muscles, to pump blood, to perform basic organic functions. I don't even know all the organs in my body; what's more, I don't know what they really do, and most importantly, how they do it?

I have two favorite questions: how? and why? "Why?" is the easier of the two. "Why?" is inextricably bound to the past, to the myriad of reasons, so the answer can always be found if you dig deep enough. "How?" is more difficult, especially as it pertains to the future and present.

In childhood, adults were divided into two types: some of them predicted a future in mathematics for me; others, a lawyer. But they all reached a unanimous consensus—the profession must be serious, make money, give socials status. "Creation?" they scoffed, "Pssh, please! Keep dreaming! That'll never work!"

After the ninth grade, I entered Economics College. At 25, I earned good money and was an excellent manager.

Now I'm 30 and I became a writer. Do I keep dreaming? Can this still work? Why did I choose this path? How can I do it?

It seems, that the process of creativity is a constant struggle between flow and chaos. But it only seems that way. Yes, flow and chaos are tentpoles of creativity; they are like its foundation, which in essence is equal to the basic building's blocks of life. At the same time, without clarity, without a precisely selected word, without a specific color, a pure note, creativity is impossible.

Creativity is continuous, endless chaos, in which everything is determent by the ability to focus and make decisions. And again, this is similar to life—daily, ordinary (in the minds of the majority) life.

Business, art, construction, sport—everything has common features, everything intersects, everywhere is the same—life, which means chaos everywhere; bravery, determination and accuracy are needed everywhere.

Why didn't we discuss these things in school or in college? All professions and trends are laden with stereotypes. Stuffed so hard that they have almost no life left. A young man comes into the profession and only by the middle of his/her life understands how much and how to shake up the shit so that he/she makes a real life appears.

But I was talking about a brain that automatically crumbles memories. I wish I could be like Proust. It is a pity, I don't have his ability to unarchive the memory. A bundle of memories, as a bundle of antique papyrus of Herculaneum, which was found under the rubble of the burned Pompeii. I take it in my hand, but I cannot unravel it. I see the shape, the color, read the title, twist it this way and that, but I enable to expand it. And if I apply too much pressure, carelessly mishandling it without due caution, it will evaporate into the dust, drugging all its letters, drawings, and colors into the ether disappearing forever, irrevocably.

How many things have I lost so irrevocably?

Proust is metaphorical Dr. Vito Mochella. Vito is a scientist. With the help of X-ray phase-contrast tomography, he reads rolls without unwrapping them. Slowly, one by one. Proust, in an absolutely unique way, known to him alone, knew how to unfold his papyri to read every second and every moment of life. I simply can't do that.
I see this Ferris wheel on the Santa Monica pier; it's without light now; I see people passing by me, mostly their pale heels and ankles; I see how they leave footprints on the wet sand, an imprint from a sneaker, an imprint from a barefoot, an imprint from a child's foot, an imprint from an adult; I see the waves erase these imprints; a damp rag on a green chalkboard after classes; I see the blue lifeguard post; I hear the blue door creak; I hear the wind, hear the waves, see the waves, hear the ocean, see the ocean; I touch the warm sand; I see the sky changes its gradient from the white color to deep blue; I see white stripes from airplanes: one, two, three, four, five, eight… eleven! Eleven lanes! They freeze in the sky like gymnasts' ribbons.

I feel the sun; it scorches my back. Especially, my lower back; it's bare; it hasn't smeared with sunscreen. It must burn. At the same time, a cold wind blows on my face and so I turn up the collar of my blue flannel shirt above. I'm cold in the front and hot in the back. If I sit facing to the ocean (now I sit sideways), the same pattern will repeat itself, only this time I will be hot on the left and cold on the right. Everything will repeat itself, just in the opposite. Does it matter? I breathe in the moist, clean ocean air; it's salty and sweet.

It's hard to think of the often-decried consequences of global pollution and excess emissions here. It's difficult to think about the harm that men do to nature. For this you need to go to India or Bali, or even better—in Kryvyi Rih, there is almost the same mess. I breathe deeply, I see clean sand and clear ocean. It seems only they exist. All this is happening to me now, but neither words nor memory are enough to keep this moment in full resolution.

Not enough focus; not enough knowledge. I breathe unconsciously, I see unconsciously, I feel unconsciously; I notice something; I notice the small specks; however, a lump, a mysterious lumpy mixture of the cold ocean, blue sky and golden sand rushes past! Smells come and go. There is the aroma of fried potatoes and semolina with milk; here, again, only the sweet-salty ocean; here, oh, some new virgin flavor, some... No, I can't put my finger on it. I perceive it unconsciously, and if I'm aware of it, I'm not able to pause, to capture it. Everything, everything comes and goes! Chaos, flows, life. Damn trains, damn wooden subway bench, damn ocean, damn Proust and all the papyri found!

What is happening now in my body? I'm deep in thought. I feel hungry. I didn't have breakfast. I got up at 6:30, or rather, woke up; I washed the dishes, dusted the furniture, vacuumed, smoked, and came here; yet I feel like I'm still sleeping. Did I even wash my face? Did I brush my teeth? I don't remember. I've been here for over an hour. Maybe two. I lost track of time. I don't want to carry my phone. I don't want to see my phone and all the contacts in it. I don't want to move, so I allow time to rush by. Keeping track of time won't help me. It won't change anything. Each second is followed by another second and these values, this projection, this process is called time, be they hours of minutes, minutes of seconds. The years. So many years. One month, three, five months. The years. So many years.

Scientists claim time doesn't exist. In the universe, it doesn't exist. How? How can that be? Why must I be tethered to time? Why do I live with time or in time, or under time? God, how do I live?

When "how?" and "why?" come together, I want to shoot myself. Psychologists, I forgot to say, argue that even within us there is no concept of time. I have no time inside of me. Okay, the universe is vast, far away. Ah. To hell with it, I'm not obligated to understand it. But me! I'm here. I am minuscule. I have all the sentience. I have only myself. I am not limitless, and I am not thousands of years old. I'm only thirty. I've been living with myself these past thirty years, so why don't I sense the lack of time within me? Subconsciously. How can I live between these two timeless spaces—my microcosm inside and macrocosm outside? Why is being between two spaces without time, even as we exist in a specific moment within the space-time continuum, so important? Why? How?

I can't write compelling farewell letters. Everything is crumpled, incomprehensible, dissolved in an instant, and I just continue to live unconsciously, moving solely on the whims of my inner being. It's already 11:30 am. At 12 pm I need to be in the apartment. Pack my stuff, wash, dry clothes and... hell, something else had to be done, but I forgot. Oh, I still have to eat. Maybe yesterday's rice? No, I don't want it. But, why not? It's only cold. I'll make it warm. This is the last day of 2018 in Santa Monica, California. I want to keep it real, full, and alive without the meddlesome nature of time, much like the universe, much like my subconscious. I wish to live without time in the eternal chaos of creative existence and whisper to the world:

I am your opus,
I am your valuable
The pure gold baby.